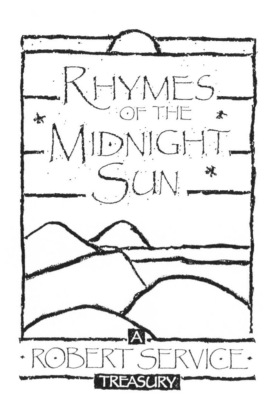

RHYMES
OF THE
MIDNIGHT
SUN

A
ROBERT SERVICE
TREASURY

RHYMES OF THE MIDNIGHT SUN

A ROBERT SERVICE TREASURY

A Lorraine Greey Book

McGraw-Hill Ryerson Limited
TORONTO    MONTREAL

**McGraw-Hill Ryerson Limited**
330 Progress Avenue
Scarborough, Ontario M1P 2Z5

**Canadian Cataloguing in Publication Data**

Service, Robert W., 1874-1958.
Rhymes of the midnight sun

ISBN 0-07-549957-6

I. Title.

PS8537.E78R49  1989    C811'.52    C89-095053-9
PR9199.3.S45R49  1989

**Produced by**
**Lorraine Greey Publications Limited**
**56 The Esplanade, Suite 303**
**Toronto, Ontario M5E 1A7**

*Poems selected by Valerie Frith*
*Designed by Holly Fisher & Associates*

Printed and bound in Canada

# Contents

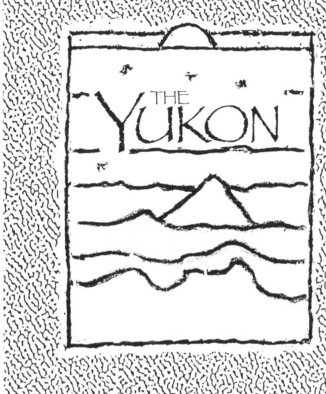

# The Spell of the Yukon

I wanted the gold, and I
    sought it;
I scrabbled and mucked
    like a slave.
Was it famine or scurvy
    — I fought it;
  I hurled my youth into a grave.
I wanted the gold, and I got it —
  Came out with a fortune last fall, —
Yet somehow life's not what I thought it,
  And somehow the gold isn't all.

No! There's the land. (Have you seen it?)
  It's the cussedest land that I know,
From the big, dizzy mountains that screen it
  To the deep, deathlike valleys below.
Some say God was tired when He made it;
  Some say it's a fine land to shun;
Maybe; but there's some as would trade it
  For no land on earth — and I'm one.

You come to get rich (damned good reason);
  You feel like an exile at first;
You hate it like hell for a season,
  And then you are worse than the worst.
It grips you like some kinds of sinning;
  It twists you from foe to a friend;
It seems it's been since the beginning;
  It seems it will be to the end.

## THE SPELL OF THE YUKON

I've stood in some mighty-mouthed hollow
    That's plumb-full of hush to the brim;
I've watched the big, husky sun wallow
    In crimson and gold, and grow dim,
Till the moon set the pearly peaks gleaming,
    And the stars tumbled out, neck and crop;
And I've thought that I surely was dreaming,
    With the peace o' the world piled on top.

The summer — no sweeter was ever;
    The sunshiny woods all athrill;
The grayling aleap in the river,
    The bighorn asleep on the hill.
The strong life that never knows harness;
    The wilds where the caribou call;
The freshness, the freedom, the farness —
    O God! how I'm stuck on it all.

The winter! the brightness that blinds you,
    The white land locked tight as a drum,
The cold fear that follows and finds you,
    The silence that bludgeons you dumb.
The snows that are older than history,
    The woods where the weird shadows slant;
The stillness, the moonlight, the mystery,
    I've bade 'em good-by — but I can't.

There's a land where the mountains are nameless,
    And the rivers all run God knows where;
There are lives that are erring and aimless,
    And deaths that just hang by a hair;

## THE SPELL OF THE YUKON

There are hardships that nobody reckons;
　　There are valleys unpeopled and still;
There's a land — oh, it beckons and beckons,
　　And I want to go back — and I will.

They're making my money diminish;
　　I'm sick of the taste of champagne.
Thank God! when I'm skinned to a finish
　　I'll pike to the Yukon again.
I'll fight — and you bet it's no sham-fight;
　　It's hell! — but I've been there before;
And it's better than this by a damsite —
　　So me for the Yukon once more.

There's gold, and it's haunting and haunting;
　　It's luring me on as of old;
Yet it isn't the gold that I'm wanting
　　So much as just finding the gold.
It's the great, big, broad land 'way up yonder,
　　It's the forests where silence has lease;
It's the beauty that thrills me with wonder,
　　It's the stillness that fills me with peace.

# The Men That Don't Fit In

There's a race of men that don't
    fit in,
A race that can't stay still;
So they break the hearts of
    kith and kin,
And they roam the world at will.
They range the field and they rove the flood,
   And they climb the mountain's crest;
Theirs is the curse of the gypsy blood,
   And they don't know how to rest.

If they just went straight they might go far;
   They are strong and brave and true;
But they're always tired of the things that are,
   And they want the strange and new.
They say: "Could I find my proper groove,
   What a deep mark I would make!"
So they chop and change, and each fresh move
   Is only a fresh mistake.

And each forgets, as he strips and runs
   With a brilliant, fitful pace,
It's the steady, quiet, plodding ones
   Who win in the lifelong race.
And each forgets that his youth has fled,
   Forgets that his prime is past,
Till he stands one day, with a hope that's dead,
   In the glare of the truth at last.

## THE MEN THAT DON'T FIT IN

He has failed, he has failed; he has missed his chance;
    He has just done things by half.
Life's been a jolly good joke on him,
    And now is the time to laugh.
Ha, ha! He is one of the Legion Lost;
    He was never meant to win;
He's a rolling stone, and it's bred in the bone;
    He's a man who won't fit in.

# The Shooting of Dan McGrew

 bunch of the boys were whooping it up in the Malamute saloon;
The kid that handles the music-box was hitting a jag-time tune;
Back of the bar, in a solo game, sat Dangerous Dan McGrew,
And watching his luck was his light-o'-love, the lady that's known as Lou.

When out of the night, which was fifty below, and into the din and the glare,
There stumbled a miner fresh from the creeks, dog-dirty, and loaded for bear.
He looked like a man with a foot in the grave and scarcely the strength of a louse,
Yet he tilted a poke of dust on the bar, and he called for drinks for the house.
There was none could place the stranger's face, though we searched ourselves for a clue;
But we drank his health, and the last to drink was Dangerous Dan McGrew.

There's men that somehow just grip your eyes, and hold them hard like a spell;
And such was he, and he looked to me like a man who had lived in hell;
With a face most hair, and the dreary stare of a dog whose day is done,

## THE SHOOTING OF DAN McGREW

As he watered the green stuff in his glass, and the
  drops fell one by one.
Then I got to figgering who he was, and wondering
  what he'd do,
And I turned my head — and there watching him
  was the lady that's known as Lou.

His eyes went rubbering round the room, and he
  seemed in a kind of daze,
Till at last that old piano fell in the way of his
  wandering gaze.
The rag-time kid was having a drink; there was no
  one else on the stool,
So the stranger stumbles across the room, and flops
  down there like a fool.
In a buckskin shirt that was glazed with dirt he sat,
  and I saw him sway;
Then he clutched the keys with his talon hands —
  my God! but that man could play.

Were you ever out in the Great Alone, when the
  moon was awful clear,
And the icy mountains hemmed you in with a
  silence you most could *hear*;
With only the howl of a timber wolf, and you
  camped there in the cold,
A half-dead thing in a stark, dead world, clean mad
  for the muck called gold;
While high overhead, green, yellow and red, the
  North Lights swept in bars? —
Then you've a hunch what the music meant . . .
  hunger and night and the stars.

And hunger not of the belly kind, that's banished
    with bacon and beans,
But the gnawing hunger of lonely men for a home
    and all that it means;
For a fireside far from the cares that are, four walls
    and a roof above;
But oh! so cramful of cosy joy, and crowned with a
    woman's love —
A woman dearer than all the world, and true as
    Heaven is true —
(God! how ghastly she looks through her rouge, —
    the lady that's known as Lou.)

Then on a sudden the music changed, so soft that
    you scarce could hear;
But you felt that your life had been looted clean of
    all that it once held dear;
That someone had stolen the woman you loved;
    that her love was a devil's lie;
That your guts were gone, and the best for you was
    to crawl away and die.
'Twas the crowning cry of a heart's despair, and it
    thrilled you through and through —
"I guess I'll make it a spread misere," said Dangerous
    Dan McGrew.

The music almost died away … then it burst like a
    pent-up flood;
And it seemed to say, "Repay, repay," and my eyes
    were blind with blood.
The thought came back of an ancient wrong, and it
    stung like a frozen lash,

And the lust awoke to kill, to kill ... then the
   music stopped with a crash,
And the stranger turned, and his eyes they burned
   in a most peculiar way;
In a buckskin shirt that was glazed with dirt he sat,
   and I saw him sway;
Then his lips went in in a kind of grin, and he spoke,
   and his voice was calm,
And "Boys," says he, "you don't know me, and
   none of you care a damn;
But I want to state, and my words are straight, and
   I'll bet my poke they're true,
That one of you is a hound of hell ... and that one
   is Dan McGrew."

Then I ducked my head, and the lights went out,
   and two guns blazed in the dark,
And a woman screamed, and the lights went up, and
   two men lay stiff and stark.
Pitched on his head, and pumped full of lead, was
   Dangerous Dan McGrew,
While the man from the creeks lay clutched to the
   breast of the lady that's known as Lou.

These are the simple facts of the case, and I guess I
   ought to know.
They say that the stranger was crazed with "hooch,"
   and I'm not denying it's so.
I'm not so wise as the lawyer guys, but strictly
   between us two —
The woman that kissed him and — pinched his
   poke — was the lady that's known as Lou.

# The Baldness of Chewed-Ear

hen Chewed-ear Jenkins got hitched up to
    Guinneyveer McGee,
His flowin' locks, ye recollect, wuz frivolous
    an' free;
But in old Hymen's jack-pot, it's a most
    amazin' thing,
Them flowin' locks jest disappeared like snow-balls in the Spring;
Jest seemed to wilt an' fade away like dead leaves in the Fall,
An' left old Chewed-ear balder than a white-washed cannon ball.

Now Missis Chewed-ear Jenkins, that wuz Guinneyveer McGee,
Wuz jest about as fine a draw as ever made a pair;
But when the boys got joshin' an' suggested it was she
That must be inflooenshul for the old man's slump in hair —
Why! Missis Chewed-ear Jenkins jest went clean up in the air.

"To demonstrate," sez she that night, "the lovin' wife I am,
I've bought a dozen bottles of Bink's Anty-Dandruff Balm.
'Twill make yer hair jest sprout an' curl like squash-vines in the sun,
An' I'm propose to sling it on till every drop is done."
That hit old Chewed-ear's funny side, so he lays back an' hollers:
"The day you raise a hair, old girl, you'll git a thousand dollars."

Now, whether 'twas the prize or not 'tis mighty hard to say,
But Chewed-ear didn't seem to have much comfort from that day.
With bottles of that dandruff dope she followed at his heels,
An' sprinkled an' massaged him even when he ate his meals.
She waked him from his beauty sleep with tender, lovin' care,
An' rubbed an' scrubbed assiduous, yet never sign of hair.

Well, naturally all the boys soon tumbled to the joke,
An' at the Wow-wow's Social 'twas Cold-deck Davis spoke:
"The little woman's working mighty hard on Chewed-ear's crown;
Let's give her for a three-fifth's share a hundred dollars down.
We stand to make five hundred clear — boys, drink in whiskey straight.
'The Chewed-ear Jenkins Hirsute Propagation Syndicate.' "

The boys wuz on, an' soon chipped in the necessary dust;
They primed up a committy to negotiate the deal;
Then Missis Jenkins yielded, bein' rather in disgust,
An' all wuz signed an' witnessed, an' invested with a seal.
They rounded up old Chewed-ear, an' they broke it what they'd done;
Allowed they'd bought an interest in his chance of raisin' hair;
They yanked his hat off anxiouslike, opinin' one by one
Their magnifyin' glasses showed fine prospects everywhere.
They bought Hairlene, an' Thatchem, an' Jay's Capillery Juice,
An' Seven Something Sisters, an' Macassar an' Bay Rum,
An' everyone insisted on his speshul right to sluice
His speshul line of lotion onto Chewed-ear's cranium.
They only got the merrier the more the old man roared,
An' shares in "Jenkins Hirsute" went sky-highin' on the board.

The Syndicate wuz hopeful that they'd demonstrate the pay,
An' Missis Jenkins laboured in her perseverin' way.
The boys discussed on "surface rights," an' "out-crops" an' so on,
An' planned to have it "crown" surveyed, an' blue prints of it drawn.
They ran a base line, sluiced an' yelled, an' everyone wuz glad,
Except the balance of the property, an' he wuz "mad."
"It gives me pain," he interjects, "to squash yer glowin' dream,
But you wuz fools when you got in on this here 'Hirsute' scheme.
You'll never raise a hair on me," when lo! that very night,
Preparin' to retire he got a most onpleasant fright:
For on that shinin' dome of his, so prominently bare,
He felt the baby outcrop of a second growth of hair.

## THE BALDNESS OF CHEWED-EAR

A thousand dollars! Sufferin' Caesar! Well, it must be saved!
He grabbed his razor recklesslike, an' shaved an' shaved an' shaved.
An' when his head was smooth again he gives a mighty sigh,
An' sneaks away, an' buys some Hair Destroyer on the sly.
So there wuz Missis Jenkins with "Restorer" wagin' fight,
An' Chewed-ear with "Destroyer" circumventin' her at night.
The battle wuz a mighty one; his nerves wuz on the strain,
An' yet in spite of all he did that hair began to gain.

The situation grew intense, so quietly one day,
He gave his share-holders the slip, an' made his get-a-way.
Jest like a criminal he skipped, an' aimed to defalcate
The Chewed-ear Jenkins Hirsute Propagation Syndicate.
His guilty secret burned him, an' he sought the city's din:
"I've got to get a wig," sez he, "to cover up my sin.
It's growin', growin' night an' day; it's most amazin' hair";
An' when he looked at it that night, he shuddered with despair,
He shuddered an' suppressed a cry at what his optics seen —
For on my word of honour, boys, that hair wuz growin' *green*.

At first he guessed he'd get some dye, an' try to dye it black;
An ' then he saw 'twas Nemmysis wuz layin' on his track.
He must jest face the music, an' confess the thing he done,
An' pay the boys an' Guinneyveer the money they had won.
An' then there came a big idee — it thrilled him like a shock.
Why not control the Syndicate by buying up the Stock?

An' so next day he hurried back with smoothly shaven pate,
An' for a hundred dollars he bought up the Syndicate.
'Twas mighty frenzied finance an' the boys set up a roar,
But "Hirsutes" from the market wuz withdrawn for evermore.
An' to this day in Nuggetsville they tell the tale how slick
The Syndicate sold out too soon, and Chewed-ear turned the trick.

# My Friends

he man above was a murderer, the man below was a thief,
And I lay there in the bunk between, ailing beyond belief,
A weary armful of skin and bone, wasted with pain and grief.

My feet were froze, and the lifeless toes were purple and green and gray;
The little flesh that clung to my bones, you could punch it in holes like clay;
The skin on my gums was a sullen black, and slowly peeling away.

I was sure enough in a direful fix, and often I wondered why
They did not take the chance that was left and leave me alone to die,
Or finish me off with a dose of dope — so utterly lost was I.

But no; they brewed me the green-spruce tea, and nursed me there like a child;
And the homicide he was good to me, and bathed my sores and smiled;
And the thief he starved that I might be fed, and his eyes were kind and mild.

## MY FRIENDS

Yet they were woefully wicked men, and often
    at night in pain
I heard the murderer speak of his deed and
    dream it over again;
I heard the poor thief sorrowing for the dead
    self he had slain.

I'll never forget that bitter dawn, so evil,
    askew and gray,
When they wrapped me round in the skins of
    beasts and they bore me to a sleigh,
And we started out with the nearest post an
    hundred miles away.

I'll never forget the trail they broke, with its
    tense, unuttered woe;
And the crunch, crunch, crunch as their
    snowshoes sank through the crust of the
    hollow snow;
And my breath would fail, and every beat of
    my heart was like a blow.

And oftentimes I would die the death, yet
    wake up to life anew;
The sun would be all ablaze on the waste, and
    the sky a blighting blue,
And the tears would rise in my snow-blind
    eyes and furrow my cheeks like dew.

And the camps we made when their strength
    outplayed and the day was pinched and wan;
And oh, the joy of that blessed halt, and how
    I did dread the dawn;
And how I hated the weary men who rose and
    dragged me on.

And oh, how I begged to rest, to rest — the
    snow was so sweet a shroud;
And oh, how I cried whey they urged me on,
    cried and cursed them aloud;
Yet on they strained, all racked and pained,
    and sorely their backs were bowed.

And then it was like a lurid dream, and I
    prayed for a swift release
From the ruthless ones who would not leave
    me to die alone in peace;
Till I wakened up and found myself at the post
    of the Mounted Police.

And there was my friend the murderer, and
    there was my friend the thief,
With bracelets of steel around their wrists,
    and wicked beyond belief;
But when they come to God's judgment seat
    — may I be allowed the brief.

# The Ballad of Salvation Bill

T was in the bleary middle of the hard-boiled
    Arctic night,
I was lonesome as a loon, so if you can,
Imagine my emotions of amazement
    and delight
When I bumped into that Missionary Man.
He was lying lost and dying in the moon's unholy leer,
And frozen from his toes to finger-tips;
The famished wolf-pack ringed him; but he didn't seem to fear,
As he pressed his ice-bound Bible to his lips.

'Twas the limit of my trap-line, with the cabin miles away,
And every step was like a stab of pain;
But I packed him like a baby, and I nursed him night and day,
Till I got him back to health and strength again.
So there we were, benighted in the shadow of the Pole,
And he might have proved a priceless little pard,
If he hadn't got to worrying about my blessed soul,
And a-quotin' me his Bible by the yard.

Now there was I, a husky guy, whose god was Nicotine.
With a "coffin-nail" a fixture in my mug;
I rolled them in the pages of a pulpwood magazine,
And hacked them with my jack-knife from the plug.
For, oh to know the bliss and glow that good tobacco means,
Just live among the everlasting ice....
So judge my horror when I found my stock of magazines
Was chewed into a chowder by the mice.

## THE BALLAD OF SALVATION BILL

A woeful week went by and not a single pill I had,
Me that would smoke my forty in a day;
I sighed, I swore, I strode the floor; I felt I would go mad:
The gospel-plugger watched me in dismay.
My brow was wet, my teeth were set, my nerves were rasping raw;
And yet that preacher couldn't understand:
So with despair I wrestled there — when suddenly I saw
The volume he was holding in his hand.

Then something snapped inside my brain, and with an evil start
The wolf-man in me woke to rabid rage.
"I saved your lousy life," says I; "so show you have a heart,
And tear me out a solitary page."
He shrank and shrivelled at my words; his face went pewter white;
'Twas just as if I'd handed him a blow;
And then ... and then he seemed to swell, and grow to Heaven's height,
And in a voice that rang he answered: "No!"

I grabbed my loaded rifle and I jabbed it to his chest:
"Come on, you shrimp, give up that Book," says I.
Well sir, he was a parson, but he stacked up with the best,
And for grit I got to hand it to the guy.
"If I should let you desecrate this Holy Word," he said,
"My soul would be eternally accurst;
So go on, Bill, I'm ready. You can pump me full of lead
And take it, but — you've got to kill me first."

Now I'm no foul assassin, though I'm full of sinful ways,
And I knew right there the fellow had me beat;
For I felt a yellow mongrel in the glory of his gaze,
And I flung my foolish firearm at his feet.

Then wearily I turned away, and dropped upon my bunk,
And there I lay and blubbered like a kid.
"Forgive me, pard," says I at last, "for acting like a skunk,
But hide the blasted rifle...." Which he did.

And he also hid his Bible, which was maybe just as well,
For the sight of all that paper gave me pain;
And there were crimson moments when I felt I'd go to hell
To have a single cigarette again.
And so I lay day after day, and brooded dark and deep,
Until one night I thought I'd end it all;
Then rough I roused the preacher, where he stretched pretending sleep,
With his map of horror turned towards the wall.

"See here, my pious pal," says I, "I've stood it long enough....
Behold! I've mixed some strychnine in a cup;
Enough to kill a dozen men — believe me it's no bluff;
Now watch me, for I'm gonna drink it up.
You've seen me bludgeoned by despair through bitter days and nights,
And now you'll see me squirming as I die.
You're not to blame, you've played the game according to your lights....
But how would Christ have played it? — Well, good-bye...."

With that I raised the deadly drink and laid it to my lips,
But he was on me with a tiger-bound;
And as we locked and reeled and rocked with wild and wicked grips,
The poison cup went crashing to the ground.
"Don't do it, Bill," he madly shrieked. "Maybe I acted wrong.
See, here's my Bible — use it as you will;
But promise me — you'll read a little as you go along....
You do! Then take it, Brother, smoke your fill."

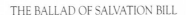

## THE BALLAD OF SALVATION BILL

And so I did. I smoked and smoked from Genesis to Job,
And as I smoked I read each blessed word;
While in the shadow of his bunk I heard him sigh and sob,
And then ... a most peculiar thing occurred.
I got to reading more and more, and smoking less and less,
Till just about the day his heart was broke,
Says I: "Here, take it back, me lad. I've had enough, I guess.
Your paper makes a mighty rotten smoke."

So then and there with plea and prayer he wrestled for my soul,
And I was racked and ravaged by regrets.
But God was good, for lo! next day there came the police patrol,
With paper for a thousand cigarettes....
So now I'm called Salvation Bill; I teach the Living Law,
And Bally-hoo the Bible with the best;
And if a guy won't listen — why, I sock him on the jaw,
And preach the Gospel sitting on his chest.

# Hobo

A father's pride I
　　used to know,
A mother's love
　　was mine;
For swinish husks
　　I let them go,
And bedded with the swine.
Since then I've come on evil days
And most of life is hell;
But even swine have winsome ways
When once you know them well.

One time I guessed I'd cease to roam,
And greet the folks again;
And so I rode the rods to home
And through the window pane
I saw them weary, worn and grey . . .
I gazed from garden gloom,
And like sweet, shiny saints were they
In that sweet, shiny room.

D'ye think I hollered out: "Hullo!"
The prodigal to play,
And eat the fatted calf? Ah no,
I cursed and ran away.
My eyes were blears of whisky tears
As to a pub I ran:
But once at least I beat the beast
And proved myself a man.

## HOBO

Oh, some day I am going back,
But I'll have gold galore;
I'll wear a suit of sober black
And knock upon the door.
I'll tell them how I've made a stake,
We'll have the grandest time....
*"Say, Mister, give a guy a break:*
*For Crissake, spare a dime."*

# The Trail of Ninety-Eight

## 1

old! We leapt from our benches. Gold! We
    sprang from our stools.
Gold! We wheeled in the furrow, fired with
    the faith of fools.
Fearless, unfound, unfitted, far from the night
    and the cold,
Heard we the clarion summons, followed the master-lure — Gold!

Men from the sands of the Sunland; men from the woods of the West;
Men from the farms and the cities, into the Northland we pressed.
Graybeards and striplings and women, good men and bad men and bold,
Leaving our homes and our loved ones, crying exultantly — "Gold!"

Never was seen such an army, pitiful, futile, unfit;
Never was seen such a spirit, manifold courage and grit.
Never has been such a cohort under one banner unrolled
As surged to the ragged-edged Arctic, urged by the archtempter — Gold.

"Farewell!" we cried to our dearests; little we cared for their tears.
"Farewell!" we cried to the humdrum and the yoke of the hireling years;
Just like a pack of school-boys, and the big crowd cheered us good-bye.
Never were hearts so uplifted, never were hopes so high.

The spectral shores flitted past us, and every whirl of the screw
Hurled us nearer to fortune, and ever we planned what we'd do —
Do with the gold when we got it — big, shiny nuggets like plums,
There in the sand of the river, gouging it out with our thumbs.

And one man wanted a castle, another a racing stud;
A third would cruise in a palace yacht like a red-necked prince of blood.
And so we dreamed and we vaunted, millionaires to a man,
Leaping to wealth in our visions long ere the trail began.

## 2

We landed in wind-swept Skagway. We joined the weltering mass,
Clamoring over their outfits, waiting to climb the Pass.
We tightened our girths and our pack-straps; we linked on the Human Chain,
Struggling up to the summit, where every step was a pain.

Gone was the joy of our faces, grim and haggard and pale;
The heedless mirth of the shipboard was changed to the care of the trail.
We flung ourselves in the struggle, packing our grub in relays,
Step by step to the summit in the bale of the winter days.

Floundering deep in the sump-holes, stumbling out again;
Crying with cold and weakness, crazy with fear and pain.
Then from the depths of our travail, ere our spirits were broke,
Grim, tenacious and savage, the lust of the trail awoke.

"Klondike or bust!" rang the slogan; every man for his own.
Oh, how we flogged the horses, staggering skin and bone!
Oh, how we cursed their weakness, anguish they could not tell,
Breaking their hearts in our passion, lashing them on till they fell!

For grub meant gold to our thinking, and all that could walk must pack;
The sheep for the shambles stumbled, each with a load on its back;
And even the swine were burdened, and grunted and squealed and rolled,
And men went mad in the moment, huskily clamoring "Gold!"

## THE TRAIL OF NINETY-EIGHT

Oh, we were brutes and devils, goaded by lust and fear!
Our eyes were strained to the summit; the weaklings dropped to the rear,
Falling in heaps by the trail-side, heart-broken, limp and wan;
But the gaps closed up in an instant, and heedless the chain went on.

Never will I forget it, there on the mountain face,
Antlike, men with their burdens, clinging in icy space;
Dogged, determined and dauntless, cruel and callous and cold,
Cursing, blaspheming, reviling, and ever that battle-cry — "Gold!"

Thus toiled we, the army of fortune, in hunger and hope and despair,
Till glacier, mountain and forest vanished, and, radiantly fair,
There at our feet lay Lake Bennett, and down to its welcome we ran:
The trail of the land was over, the trail of the water began.

## 3

We built our boats and we launched them. Never has been such a fleet;
A packing-case for a bottom, a mackinaw for a sheet.
Shapeless, grotesque, lopsided, flimsy, makeshift and crude,
Each man after his fashion builded as best he could.

Each man worked like a demon, as prow to rudder we raced;
The winds of the Wild cried "Hurry!" the voice of the waters, "Haste!"
We hated those driving before us; we dreaded those pressing behind;
We cursed the slow current that bore us; we prayed to the God of the wind.

Spring! and the hillsides flourished, vivid in jewelled green;
Spring! and our hearts' blood nourished envy and hatred and spleen.
Little cared we for the Spring-birth; much cared we to get on —
Stake in the Great White Channel, stake ere the best be gone.

## THE TRAIL OF NINETY-EIGHT

The greed of the gold possessed us; pity and love were forgot;
Covetous visions obsessed us; brother with brother fought.
Partner with partner wrangled, each one claiming his due;
Wrangled and halved their outfits, sawing their boats in two.

Thuswise we voyaged Lake Bennett, Tagish, then Windy Arm,
Sinister, savage and baleful, boding us hate and harm.
Many a scow was shattered there on that iron shore;
Many a heart was broken straining at sweep and oar.

We roused Lake Marsh with a chorus, we drifted many a mile;
There was the canyon before us — cave-like its dark defile;
The shores swept faster and faster; the river narrowed to wrath;
Waters that hissed disaster reared upright in our path.

Beneath us the green tumult churning, above us the cavernous gloom;
Around us, swift twisting and turning, the black, sullen walls of a tomb.
We spun like a chip in a mill-race; our hearts hammered under the test;
Then — oh, the relief on each chill face! — we soared into sunlight and rest.

Hand sought for hand on the instant. Cried we, "Our troubles are o'er!"
Then, like a rumble of thunder, heard we a canorous roar.
Leaping and boiling and seething, saw we a cauldron afume;
There was the rage of the rapids, there was the menace of doom.

The river springs like a racer, sweeps through a gash in the rock;
Butts at the boulder-ribbed bottom, staggers and rears at the shock;
Leaps like a terrified monster, writhes in its fury and pain;
Then with the crash of a demon springs to the onset again.

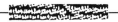

Dared we that ravening terror; heard we its din in our ears;
Called on the Gods of our fathers, juggled forlorn with our fears;
Sank to our waists in its fury, tossed to the sky like a fleece;
Then, when our dread was the greatest, crashed into safety and peace.

But what of the others that followed, losing their boats by the score?
Well could we see them and hear them, strung down that desolate shore.
What of the poor souls that perished? Little of them shall be said —
On to the Golden Valley, pause not to bury the dead.

Then there were days of drifting, breezes soft as a sigh;
Night trailed her robe of jewels over the floor of the sky.
The moonlit stream was a python, silver, sinuous, vast,
That writhed on a shroud of velvet — well, it was done at last.

There were the tents of Dawson, there the scar of the slide;
Swiftly we poled o'er the shallows, swiftly leapt o'er the side.
Fires fringed the mouth of Bonanza; sunset gilded the dome;
The test of the trail was over — thank God, thank God, we were Home!

# The Cremation of Sam McGee

*There are strange things done in the midnight sun*
*By the men who moil for gold;*
*The Arctic trails have their secret tales*
*That would make your blood run cold;*
*The Northern Lights have seen queer sights,*
*But the queerest they ever did see*
*Was that night on the marge of Lake Lebarge*
*I cremated Sam McGee.*

Now Sam McGee was from Tennessee, where the cotton blooms and blows.
Why he left his home in the South to roam 'round the Pole, God only knows.
He was always cold, but the land of gold seemed to hold him like a spell;
Though he'd often say in his homely way that "he'd sooner live in hell."

On a Christmas Day we were mushing our way over the Dawson trail.
Talk of your cold! through the parka's fold it stabbed like a driven nail.
If our eyes we'd close, then the lashes froze till sometimes we couldn't see;
It wasn't much fun, but the only one to whimper was Sam McGee.

And that very night, as we lay packed tight in our robes beneath the snow,
And the dogs were fed, and the stars o'erhead were dancing heel and toe,
He turned to me, and "Cap," says he, "I'll cash in this trip, I guess;
And if I do, I'm asking that you won't refuse my last request."

Well, he seemed so low that I couldn't say no; then he says with a sort
  of moan:
"It's the cursèd cold, and it's got right hold till I'm chilled clean through
  to the bone.

Yet 'tain't being dead — it's my awful dread of the icy grave that pains;
So I want you to swear that, foul or fair, you'll cremate my last remains."

A pal's last need is a thing to heed, so I swore I would not fail;
And we started on at the streak of dawn; but God! he looked ghastly pale.
He crouched on the sleigh, and he raved all day of his home in Tennessee;
And before nightfall a corpse was all that was left of Sam McGee.

There wasn't a breath in that land of death, and I hurried, horror-driven,
With a corpse half hid that I couldn't get rid, because of a promise given;
It was lashed to the sleigh, and it seemed to say: "You may tax your brawn
    and brains,
But you promised true, and it's up to you to cremate those last remains."

Now a promise made is a debt unpaid, and the trail has its own stern code.
In the days to come, though my lips were dumb, in my heart how I cursed
    that load.
In the long, long night, by the lone firelight, while the huskies, round in
    a ring,
Howled out their woes to the homeless snows — O God! how I loathed
    the thing.

And every day that quiet clay seemed to heavy and heavier grow;
And on I went, though the dogs were spent and the grub was getting low;
The trail was bad, and I felt half mad, but I swore I would not give in;
And I'd often sing to the hateful thing, and it hearkened with a grin.

Till I came to the marge of Lake Lebarge, and a derelict there lay;
It was jammed in the ice, but I saw in a trice it was called the "Alice May."
And I looked at it, and I thought a bit, and I looked at my frozen chum;
Then "Here," said I with a sudden cry, "is my cre-ma-tor-eum."

## THE CREMATION OF SAM McGEE

Some planks I tore from the cabin floor, and I lit the boiler fire;
Some coal I found that was lying around, and I heaped the fuel higher;
The flames just soared, and the furnace roared — such a blaze you seldom see;
And I burrowed a hole in the glowing coal, and I stuffed in Sam McGee.

Then I made a hike, for I didn't like to hear him sizzle so;
And the heavens scowled, and the huskies howled, and the wind began
    to blow.
It was icy cold, but the hot sweat rolled down my cheeks, and I don't
    know why;
And the greasy smoke in an inky cloak went streaking down the sky.

I do not know how long in the snow I wrestled with grisly fear;
But the stars came out and they danced about ere again I ventured near;
I was sick with dread, but I bravely said: "I'll just take a peep inside.
I guess he's cooked, and it's time I looked"; . . . then the door I opened wide.

And there sat Sam, looking cool and calm, in the heart of the furnace roar;
And he wore a smile you could see a mile, and he said: "Please close that door.
It's fine in here, but I greatly fear you'll let in the cold and storm —
Since I left Plumtree, down in Tennessee, it's the first time I've been warm."

*There are strange things done in the midnight sun*
    *By the men who moil for gold;*
*The Arctic trails have their secret tales*
    *That would make your blood run cold;*
*The Northern Lights have seen queer sights,*
    *But the queerest they ever did see*
*Was that night on the marge of Lake Lebarge*
    *I cremated Sam McGee.*

# Heart o' the North

nd when I come to
the dim trail-end,
I who have been
Life's rover,
This is all I would
ask, my friend,
Over and over and over:

A little space on a stony hill
With never another near me,
Sky o' the North that's vast and still,
With a single star to cheer me;

Star that gleams on a moss-grey stone
Graven by those who love me —
There would I lie alone, alone,
With a single pine above me;

Pine that the north wind whinnys through —
Oh, I have been Life's lover!
But there I'd lie and listen to
Eternity passing over.

# The Ballad of One-Eyed Mike

his is the tale that was told to
me by the man with the
crystal eye,
As I smoked my pipe in the
camp-fire light, and the
Glories swept the sky;
As the Northlights gleamed and curved and streamed,
and the bottle of "hooch" was dry.

A man once aimed that my life be shamed, and
  wrought me a deathly wrong;
I vowed one day I would well repay, but the heft of
  his hate was strong.
He thonged me East and he thonged me West; he
  harried me back and forth,
Till I fled in fright from his peerless spite to the
  bleak, bald-headed North.

And there I lay, and for many a day I hatched plan
  after plan,
For a golden haul of the wherewithal to crush and
  to kill my man;
And there I strove, and there I clove through the
  drift of icy streams;
And there I fought, and there I sought for the pay-
  streak of my dreams.

So twenty years, with their hopes and fears and
    smiles and tears and such,
Went by and left me long bereft of hope of the
    Midas touch;
About as fat as a chancel rat, and lo! despite my
    will,
In the weary fight I had clean lost sight of the man
    I sought to kill.

'Twas so far away, that evil day when I prayed the
    Prince of Gloom
For the savage strength and the sullen length of life
    to work his doom.
Nor sign nor word had I seen or heard, and it
    happed so long ago;
My youth was gone and my memory wan, and I
    willed it even so.

It fell one night in the waning light by the Yukon's
    oily flow,
I smoked and sat as I marvelled at the sky's port-
    winey glow;
Till it paled away to an absinthe gray, and the river
    seemed to shrink,
All wobbly flakes and wriggling snakes and goblin
    eyes a-wink.

'Twas weird to see and it 'wildered me in a queer,
    hypnotic dream,
Till I saw a spot like an inky blot come floating
    down the stream;

## THE BALLAD OF ONE-EYED MIKE

It bobbed and swung; it sheered and hung; it romped
    round in a ring;
It seemed to play in a tricksome way; it sure was a
    merry thing.

In freakish flights strange oily lights came fluttering
    round its head,
Like butterflies of a monster size — then I knew it
    for the Dead.
Its face was rubbed and slicked and scrubbed as
    smooth as a shaven pate;
In the silver snakes that the water makes it gleamed
    like a dinner-plate.

It gurgled near, and clear and clear and large and
    large it grew;
It stood upright in a ring of light and it looked me
    through and through.
It weltered round with a woozy sound, and ere I
    could retreat,
With the witless roll of a sodden soul it wantoned
    to my feet.

And here I swear by this Cross I wear, I heard that
    "floater" say:
"I am the man from whom you ran, the man you
    sought to slay.
That you may note and gaze and gloat and say
    'Revenge is sweet,'
In the grit and grime of the river's slime I am rotting
    at your feet.

"The ill we rue we must e'en undo, though it rive us
 bone from bone;
So it came about that I sought you out, for I prayed
 I might atone.
I did you wrong, and for long and long I sought
 where you might live;
And now you're found, though I'm dead and
 drowned, I beg you to forgive."

So sad it seemed, and its cheek-bones gleamed, and
 its fingers flicked the shore;
And it lapped and lay in a weary way, and its hands
 met to implore;
That I gently said: "Poor, restless dead, I would
 never work you woe;
Though the wrong you rue you can ne'er undo, I
 forgave you long ago."

Then, wonder-wise, I rubbed my eyes and I woke
 from a horrid dream.
The moon rode high in the naked sky, and
 something bobbed in the stream.
It held my sight in a patch of light, and then it
 sheered from the shore;
It dipped and sank by a hollow bank, and I never
 saw it more.

*This was the tale he told to me, that man so warped
 and gray,
Ere he slept and dreamed, and the camp-fire
 gleamed in his eye in a wolfish way —
That crystal eye that raked the sky in the weird
 Auroral ray.*

# The Parson's Son

his is the song of the parson's son, as he squats in his shack alone,
On the wild, weird nights, when the Northern Lights shoot up from the frozen zone,
And it's sixty below, and couched in the snow the hungry huskies moan:

"I'm one of the Arctic brotherhood, I'm an old-time pioneer.
I came with the first — O God! how I've cursed this Yukon — but still I'm here.
I've sweated athirst in its summer heat, I've frozen and starved in its cold;
I've followed my dreams by its thousand streams, I've toiled and moiled for its gold.

"Look at my eyes — been snow-blind twice; look where my foot's half gone;
And that gruesome scar on my left cheek, where the frost-fiend bit to the bone.
Each one a brand of this devil's land, where I've played and I've lost the game,
A broken wreck with a craze for 'hooch,' and never a cent to my name.

## THE PARSON'S SON

"This mining is only a gamble; the worst is as
    good as the best;
I was in with the bunch and I might have
    come out right on top with the rest;
With Cormack, Ladue and Macdonald — O
    God! but it's hell to think
Of the thousands and thousands I've
    squandered on cards and women and drink.

"In the early days we were just a few, and we
    hunted and fished around,
Nor dreamt by our lonely camp-fires of the
    wealth that lay under the ground.
We traded in skins and whiskey, and I've often
    slept under the shade
Of that lone birch tree on Bonanza, where the
    first big find was made.

"We were just like a great big family, and every
    man had his squaw,
And we lived such a wild, free, fearless life
    beyond the pale of the law;
Till sudden there came a whisper, and it
    maddened us every man,
And I got in on Bonanza before the big rush
    began.

"Oh, those Dawson days, and the sin and the
    blaze, and the town all open wide!
(If God made me in His likeness, sure He let
    the devil inside.)

THE PARSON'S SON

But we all were mad, both the good and the
    bad, and as for the women, well —
No spot on the map in so short a space has
    hustled more souls to hell.

"Money was just like dirt there, easy to get
    and to spend.
I was all caked in on a dance-hall jade, but she
    shook me in the end.

# The Ballad of Blasphemous Bill

I took a contract to bury the body of blasphemous
    Bill MacKie,
Whenever, wherever or whatsoever the manner
    of death he die —
Whether he die in the light o' day or under the
    peak-faced moon;
In cabin or dance-hall, camp or dive, mucklucks or patent shoon;
On velvet tundra or virgin peak, by glacier, drift or draw;
In muskeg hollow or canyon gloom, by avalanche, fang or claw;
By battle, murder or sudden wealth, by pestilence, hooch or lead —
I swore on the Book I would follow and look till I found my tombless dead.

For Bill was a dainty kind of cuss, and his mind was mighty sot
On a dinky patch with flowers and grass in a civilized bone-yard lot.
And where he died or how he died, it didn't matter a damn
So long as he had a grave with frills and a tombstone "epigram."
So I promised him, and he paid the price in good cheechako coin
(Which the same I blowed in that very night down in the Tenderloin).
Then I painted a three-foot slab of pine: "Here lies poor Bill MacKie,"
And I hung it up on my cabin wall and I waited for Bill to die.

Years passed away, and at last one day came a squaw with a story strange,
Of a long-deserted line of traps 'way back of the Bighorn range;
Of a little hut by the great divide, and a white man stiff and still,
Lying there by his lonesome self, and I figured it must be Bill.
So I thought of the contract I'd made with him, and I took down from
   the shelf
The swell black box with the silver plate he'd picked out for hisself;
And I packed it full of grub and "hooch," and I slung it on the sleigh;
Then I harnessed up my team of dogs and was off at dawn of day.

## THE BALLAD OF BLASPHEMOUS BILL

You know what it's like in the Yukon wild when it's sixty-nine below;
When the ice-worms wriggle their purple heads through the crust of the
   pale blue snow;
When the pine-trees crack like little guns in the silence of the wood,
And the icicles hang down like tusks under the parka hood;
When the stove-pipe smoke breaks sudden off, and the sky is weirdly lit,
And the careless feel of a bit of steel burns like a red-hot spit;
When the mercury is a frozen ball, and the frost-fiend stalks to kill —
Well, it was just like that that day when I set out to look for Bill.

Oh, the awful hush that seemed to crush me down on every hand,
As I blundered blind with a trail to find through that blank and bitter land;
Half dazed, half crazed in the winter wild, with its grim heart-breaking woes,
And the ruthless strife for a grip on life that only the sourdough knows!
North by the compass, North I pressed; river and peak and plain
Passed like a dream I slept to lose and I waked to dream again.

River and plain and mighty peak — and who could stand unawed?
As their summits blazed, he could stand undazed at the foot of the throne
   of God.
North, aye, North, through a land accurst, shunned by the scouring brutes,
And all I heard was my own harsh word and the whine of the malamutes,
Till at last I came to a cabin squat, built in the side of a hill,
And I burst in the door, and there on the floor, frozen to death, lay Bill.

Ice, white ice, like a winding-sheet, sheathing each smoke-grimed wall;
Ice on the stove-pipe, ice on the bed, ice gleaming over all;
Sparkling ice on the dead man's chest, glittering ice in his hair,
Ice on his fingers, ice in his heart, ice in his glassy stare;
Hard as a log and trussed like a frog, with his arms and legs outspread.
I gazed at the coffin I'd brought for him, and I gazed at the gruesome dead,
And at last I spoke: "Bill liked his joke; but still, goldarn his eyes,
A man had ought to consider his mates in the way he goes and dies."

## THE BALLAD OF BLASPHEMOUS BILL

Have you ever stood in an Arctic hut in the shadow of the Pole,
With a little coffin six by three and a grief you can't control?
Have you ever sat by a frozen corpse that looks at you with a grin,
And that seems to say: "You may try all day, but you'll never jam me in"?
I'm not a man of the quitting kind, but I never felt so blue
As I sat there gazing at that stiff and studying what I'd do.
Then I rose and I kicked off the husky dogs that were nosing round about,
And I lit a roaring fire in the stove, and I started to thaw Bill out.

Well, I thawed and thawed for thirteen days, but it didn't seem no good;
His arms and legs stuck out like pegs, as if they was made of wood.
Till at last I said: "It ain't no use — he's froze too hard to thaw;
He's obstinate, and he won't lie straight, so I guess I got to — *saw*."
So I sawed off poor Bill's arms and legs, and I laid him snug and straight
In the little coffin he picked hisself, with the dinky silver plate,
And I came nigh near to shedding a tear as I nailed him safely down;
Then I stowed him away in my Yukon sleigh, and I started back to town.

So I buried him as the contract was in a narrow grave and deep,
And there he's waiting the Great Clean-up, when the Judgment sluice-
  heads sweep;
And I smoke my pipe and I meditate in the light of the Midnight Sun,
And sometimes I wonder if they *was*, the awful things I done.
And as I sit and the parson talks, expounding of the Law,
I often think of poor old Bill — *and how hard he was to saw.*

# Dark Pine

f my life-force, by
death decree,
Could find green
haven in a tree,
And there in peace
untroubled years
Could dream, immune from toil and tears,
Though I'm a lover of all trees
I would not favour one of these . . .

I would not choose a brittle palm
Beside a sea of senile calm;
Or willow droopily adream
Above bright babble of a stream.
No cypress would inhibit me
With dark and dour austerity;
Nor olive, shattering the light,
Nor poplar, purple in the night.
The sanctuary of my search
Would not be oak, nor ash, nor birch:
Ah no! Their comfort I decline, —
Let my life-force pervade a Pine.

Aye, when my soul shall sally forth
Let it be to the naked North,
And in a lone pine desolate
Achieve its fit and final fate;
A pine by arctic tempest torn,
Snow-scourged, wind-savaged and forlorn;

## DARK PINE

A viking trunk, a warrior tree,
A hostage to dark destiny
Of iron earth and icy sky,
That valiantly disdains to die.

There is the home where I would bide,
If trees like men had souls inside, —
Which is, of course, a fantasy
None could conceive but dolts like me ...
Let others vision Heaven's gate,
Dark Pine, I dream for me you wait.

# Lucille

Of course you've heard
    of the *Nancy Lee*,
    and how she sailed
    away
On her famous quest
    of the Arctic flea,
  to the wilds of Hudson's Bay?
For it was a foreign Prince's whim to collect
  this tiny cuss,
And a golden quid was no more to him than a
  copper to coves like us.
So we sailed away and our hearts were gay
  as we gazed on the gorgeous scene;
And we laughed with glee as we caught the
  flea of the wolf and the wolverine;
Yea, our hearts were light as the parasite of
  the ermine rat we slew,
And the great musk ox, and the silver fox, and
  the moose and the caribou.
And we laughed with zest as the insect pest of
  the marmot crowned our zeal,
And the wary mink and the wily "link," and
  the walrus and the seal.
And with eyes aglow on the scornful snow we
  danced a rigadoon,
Round the lonesome lair of the Arctic hare,
  by the light of the silver moon.

But the time was nigh to homeward hie, when,
  imagine our despair!
For the best of the lot we hadn't got — the
  flea of the polar bear.

## LUCILLE

Oh, his face was long and his breath was
    strong, as the Skipper he says to me:
"I wants you to linger 'ere, my lad, by the
    shores of the Hartic Sea;
I wants you to 'unt the polar bear the
    perishin' winter through,
And if flea ye find of its breed and kind,
    there's a 'undred quid for you."
But I shook my head: "No, Cap," I said; "it's
    yourself I'd like to please,
But I tells ye flat I wouldn't do that if ye went
    on yer bended knees."
Then the Captain spat in the seething brine,
    and he says: "Good luck to you,
If it can't be did for a 'undred quid, supposin'
    we call it two?"
So that was why they said good-by, and they
    sailed and left me there —
Alone, alone in the Arctic Zone to hunt for
    the polar bear.

Oh, the days were slow and packed with woe,
    till I thought they would never end;
And I used to sit when the fire was lit, with
    my pipe for my only friend.
And I tried to sing some rollicky thing, but my
    song broke off in a prayer,
And I'd drowse and dream by the driftwood
    gleam; I'd dream of a polar bear;
I'd dream of a cloudlike polar bear that blotted
    the stars on high,
With ravenous jaws and flenzing claws, and
    the flames of hell in his eye.

## LUCILLE

And I'd trap around on the frozen ground, as a
    proper hunter ought,
And beasts I'd find of every kind, but never
    the one I sought.
Never a track in the white ice-pack that
    humped and heaved and flawed,
Till I came to think: "Why, strike me pink! if
    the creature ain't a fraud."
And then one night in the waning light, as I
    hurried home to sup,
I hears a roar by the cabin door, and a great
    white hulk heaves up.
So my rifle flashed, and a bullet crashed; dead,
    dead as a stone fell he,
And I gave a cheer, for there in his ear —
    Gosh ding me! — a tiny flea.

At last, at last! Oh, I clutched it fast, and I
    gazed on it with pride;
And I thrust it into a biscuit-tin, and I shut it
    safe inside;
With a lid of glass for the light to pass, and
    space to leap and play;
Oh, it kept alive; yea, seemed to thrive, as I
    watched it night and day.
And I used to sit and sing to it, and I shielded
    it from harm,
And many a hearty feed it had on the heft of
    my hairy arm.
For you'll never know in that land of snow
    how lonesome a man can feel;
So I made a fuss of the little cuss, and I
    christened it "Lucille."
But the longest winter has its end, and the ice
    went out to sea,

## LUCILLE

And I saw one day a ship in the bay, and there
    was the *Nancy Lee*.
So a boat was lowered and I went aboard, and
    they opened wide their eyes —
Yes, they gave a cheer when the truth was
    clear, and they saw my precious prize.
And then it was all like a giddy dream; but to
    cut my story short,
We sailed away on the fifth of May to the
    foreign Prince's court;
To a palmy land and a palace grand, and the
    little Prince was there,
And a fat Princess in a satin dres with a crown
    of gold on her hair.
And they showed me into a shiny room, just
    him and her and me,
And the Prince he was pleased and friendly-
    like, and he calls for drinks for three.
And I shows them my battered biscuit-tin, and
    I makes my modest spiel,
And they laughed, they did, when I opened
    the lid, and out there popped Lucille.

Oh, the Prince was glad, I could soon see that,
    and the Princess she was too;
And Lucille waltzed round on the tablecloth
    as she often used to do.
And the Prince pulled out a purse of gold, and
    he put it in my hand;
And he says: "It was worth all that, I'm told,
    to stay in that nasty land."
And then he turned with a sudden cry, and he
    clutched at his royal beard;
And the Princess screamed, and well she might
    — for Lucille had disappeared.

# LUCILLE

"She must be here," said his Noble Nibs, so we
    hunted all around;
Oh, we searched that place, but never a trace
    of the little beast we found.
So I shook my head, and I glumly said: "Gol
    darn the saucy cuss!
It's mighty queer, but she isn't here; so . . .
    she must be on one of us.
You'll pardon me if I make so free, but —
    there's just one thing to do:
If you'll kindly go for a half a mo' I'll search
    me garments through."
Then all alone on the shiny throne I stripped
    from head to heel;
In vain, in vain; it was very plain that I hadn't
    got Lucille.
So I garbed again, and I told the Prince, and
    he scratched his august head;
"I suppose if she hasn't selected you, it must
    be me," he said.
So *he* retired; but he soon came back, and his
    features showed distress:
"Oh, it isn't you and it isn't me." . . . Then we
    looked at the Princess.
So *she* retired; and we heard a scream, and she
    opened wide the door;
And her fingers twain were pinched to pain,
    but a radiant smile she wore:
"It's here," she cries, "our precious prize. Oh, I
    found it right away . . . ."
Then I ran to her with a shout of joy, but I
    choked with a wild dismay.
I clutched the back of the golden throne, and
    the room began to reel . . .
What she held to me was, ah yes! a flea, but
    . . . *it wasn't my Lucille.*

# The Ballad of the Ice-Worm Cocktail

o Dawson Town came Percy Brown
  from London on the Thames.
A pane of glass was in his eye, and
  stockings on his stems.
Upon the shoulder of his coat a
  leather pad he wore,
To rest his deadly rifle when it wasn't seeking gore;
The which it must have often been, for Major Percy Brown,
According to his story was a hunter of renown,
Who in the Murrumbidgee wilds had stalked the kangaroo
And killed the cassowary on the plains of Timbuctoo.
And now the Arctic fox he meant to follow to its lair,
And it was also his intent to beard the Arctic hare....
Which facts concerning Major Brown I merely tell because
I fain would have you know him for the Nimrod that he was.

Now Skipper Grey and Deacon White were sitting in the shack,
And sampling of the whisky that pertained to Sheriff Black.
Said Skipper Grey: "I want to say a word about this Brown:
The piker's sticking out his chest as if he owned the town."
Said Sheriff Black: "He has no lack of frigorated cheek;
He called himself a Sourdough when he'd just been here a week."
Said Deacon White: "Methinks you're right, and so I have a plan
By which I hope to prove to-night the mettle of the man.
Just meet me where the hooch-bird sings, and though our ways be rude
We'll make a *proper* Sourdough of this Piccadilly dude."

Within the Malamute Saloon were gathered all the gang;
The fun was fast and furious, and loud the hooch-bird sang.
In fact the night's hilarity had almost reached its crown,
When into its storm-centre breezed the gallant Major Brown

## THE BALLAD OF THE ICE-WORM COCKTAIL

And at the apparition, with its glass eye and plus-fours,
From fifty alcoholic throats resounded fifty roars.
With shouts of stark amazement and with whoops of sheer delight,
They surged around the stranger, but the first was Deacon White.
"We welcome you," he cried aloud, "to this the Great White Land.
The Arctic Brotherhood is proud to grip you by the hand.
Yea, sportsman of the bull-dog breed, from trails of far away,
To Yukoners this is indeed a memorable day.
Our jubilation to express, vocabularies fail....
Boys, hail the Great Cheechako!" And the boys responded: "Hail!"

"And now," continued Deacon White to blushing Major Brown,
"Behold assembled the *eelight* and cream of Dawson Town.
And one ambition fills their hearts and makes their bosoms glow —
They want to make you, honoured sir, a *bony feed* Sourdough.
The same, some say, is one who's seen the Yukon ice go out,
But most profound authorities the definition doubt.
And to the genial notion of this meeting, Major Brown,
A Sourdough is a guy who drinks ... an ice-worm cocktail down."

"By Gad!" responded Major Brown, "that's ripping, don't you know.
I've always felt I'd like to be a *certified* Sourdough.
And though I haven't any doubt your Winter's awf'ly nice,
Mayfair, I fear, may miss me ere the break-up of your ice.
Yet (pray excuse my ignorance of matters such as these)
A cocktail I can understand — but what's an ice-worm, please?"
Said Deacon White: "It is not strange that you should fail to know,
Since ice-worms are peculiar to the Mountain of Blue Snow.
Within the Polar rim it rears, a solitary peak,
And in the smoke of early Spring (a spectacle unique)
Like flame it leaps upon the sight and thrills you through and through,
For though its cone is piercing white, its base is blazing blue.
Yet all is clear as you draw near — for coyly peering out
Are hosts and hosts of tiny worms, each indigo of snout.

And as no nourishment they find, to keep themselves alive
They masticate each other's tails, till just the Tough survive.
Yet on this stern and Spartan fare so rapidly they grow,
That some attain six inches by the melting of the snow.
Then when the tundra glows to green and nigger heads appear,
They burrow down and are not seen until another year."

"A toughish yarn," laughed Major Brown, "as well you may admit.
I'd like to see this little beast before I swallow it."
" 'Tis easy done," said Deacon White. "Ho! Barman, haste and bring
Us forth some pickled ice-worms of the vintage of last Spring."
But sadly still was Barman Bill, then sighed as one bereft:
"There's been a run on cocktails, Boss; there ain't an ice-worm left.
Yet wait.... By gosh! it seems to me that some of extra size
Were picked and put away to show the scientific guys."

Then deeply in a drawer he sought, and there he found a jar,
The which with due and proper pride he put upon the bar;
And in it, wreathed in queasy rings, or rolled into a ball,
A score of grey and greasy things were drowned in alcohol.
Their bellies were a bilious blue, their eyes a bulbous red;
The backs were grey, and gross were they, and hideous of head.
And when with gusto and a fork the barman speared one out,
It must have gone four inches from its tail-tip to its snout.
Cried Deacon White with deep delight: "Say, isn't that a beaut?"
"I think it is," sniffed Major Brown, "a most disgustin' brute.
Its very sight gives me the pip. I'll bet my bally hat,
You're only spoofin' me, old chap. You'll never swallow that."
"The hell I won't!" said Deacon White. "Hey! Bill, that fellow's fine.
Fix up four ice-worm cocktails, and just put that wop in mine."

## THE BALLAD OF THE ICE-WORM COCKTAIL

So Barman Bill got busy, and with sacerdotal air
His art's supreme achievement he proceeded to prepare.
His silver cups, like sickle moon, went waving to and fro,
And four celestial cocktails soon were shining in a row.
And in the starry depths of each, artistically piled,
A fat and juicy ice-worm raised its mottled mug and smiled.
Then closer pressed the peering crowd, suspended was the fun,
As Skipper Grey in courteous way said: "Stranger, please take one."
But with a gesture of disgust the Major shook his head.
"You can't bluff me. You'll never drink that ghastly thing," he said.
"You'll see all right," said Deacon White, and held his cocktail high,
Till its ice-worm seemed to wiggle, and to wink a wicked eye.
Then Skipper Grey and Sheriff Black each lifted up a glass,
While through the tense and quiet crowd a tremor seemed to pass.
"Drink, Stranger, drink," boomed Deacon White. "Proclaim you're
    of the best,
A doughty Sourdough who has passed the Ice-worm Cocktail Test."
And at these words, with all eyes fixed on gaping Major Brown,
Like a libation to the gods, each dashed his cocktail down.
The Major gasped with horror as the trio smacked their lips.
He twiddled at his eye-glass with unsteady finger-tips.
Into his starry cocktail with a look of woe he peered,
And its ice-worm, to his thinking, most incontinently leered.
Yet on him were a hundred eyes, though no one spoke aloud,
For hushed wth expectation was the waiting, watching crowd.
The Major's fumbling hand went forth — the gang prepared to cheer;
The Major's falt'ring hand went back, the mob prepared to jeer.
The Major gripped his gleaming glass and laid it to his lips,
And as despairfully he took some nauseated sips,
From out its coil of crapulence the ice-worm raised its head;
Its muzzle was a murky blue, its eyes a ruby red.
And then a roughneck bellowed forth: "This stiff comes here and struts,
As if he'd bought the blasted North — jest let him show his guts."
And with a roar the mob proclaimed: "Cheechako, Major Brown,
Reveal that you're of Sourdough stuff, and drink your cocktail down."

### THE BALLAD OF THE ICE-WORM COCKTAIL

The Major took another look, then quickly closed his eyes,
For even as he raised his glass he felt his gorge arise.
Aye, even though his sight was sealed, in fancy he could see
That grey and greasy thing that reared and sneered in mockery.
Yet round him ringed the callous crowd — and how they seemed to gloat!
It must be done.... He swallowed hard.... The brute was at his throat.
He choked ... he gulped.... Thank God! at last he'd got the horror down.
Then from the crowd went up a roar: "Hooray for Sourdough Brown!"
With shouts they raised him shoulder high, and gave a rousing cheer,
But though they praised him to the sky the Major did not hear.
Amid their demonstrative glee delight he seemed to lack;
Indeed it almost seemed that he — was "keeping something back."
A clammy sweat was on his brow, and pallid as a sheet:
"I feel I must be going now," he'd plaintively repeat.
Aye, though with drinks and smokes galore, they tempted him to stay,
With sudden bolt he gained the door, and made his get-away.

And ere next night his story was the talk of Dawson Town,
But gone and reft of glory was the wrathful Major Brown;
For the ice-worm (so they told him) of such formidable size
Was — *a stick of stained spaghetti with two red ink spots for eyes.*

# The Ballad of the Black Fox Skin

## 1

here was Claw-fingered
Kitty and Windy Ike
living the life of
shame,
When unto them in
the Long, Long
Night came the man-who-had-no-name;
Bearing his prize of a black fox pelt, out of the
Wild he came.

His cheeks were blanched as the flume-head
foam when the brown spring freshets flow;
Deep in their dark, sin-calcined pits were his
sombre eyes aglow;
They knew him far for the fitful man who spat
forth blood on the snow.

"Did ever you see such a skin?" quoth he;
"there's nought in the world so fine —
Such fullness of fur as black as the night, such
lustre, such size, such shine;
It's life to a one-lunged man like me; it's
London, it's women, it's wine.

"The Moose-hides called it the devil-fox, and
swore that no man could kill;
That he who hunted it, soon or late, must
surely suffer some ill;

But I laughed at them and their old squaw-
    tales. Ha! Ha! I'm laughing still.

"For look ye, the skin — it's as smooth as sin,
    and black as the core of the Pit.
By gun or by trap, whatever the hap, I swore
    I would capture it;
By star and by star afield and afar, I hunted
    and would not quit.

"For the devil-fox, it was swift and sly, and it
    seemed to fleer at me;
I would wake in fright by the camp-fire light
    hearing its evil glee;
Into my dream its eyes would gleam, and its
    shadow would I see.

"It sniffed and ran from the ptarmigan I had
    poisoned to excess;
Unharmed it sped from my wrathful lead
    ('twas as if I shot by guess);
Yet it came by night in the stark moonlight to
    mock at my weariness.

"I tracked it up where the mountains hunch
    like the vertebrae of the world;
I tracked it down to the death-still pits where
    the avalanche is hurled;
From the glooms to the sacerdotal snows,
    where the carded clouds are curled.

"From the vastitudes where the world protrudes
    through clouds like seas up-shoaled,
I held its track till it led me back to the land
    I had left of old —
The land I had looted many moons. I was
    weary and sick and cold.

"I was sick, soul-sick, of the futile chase, and
    there and then I swore
The foul fiend fox might scathless go, for I
    would hunt no more;
Then I rubbed mine eyes in a vast surprise —
    it stood by my cabin door.

"A rifle raised in the wraith-like gloom, and a
    vengeful shot that sped;
A howl that would thrill a cream-faced corpse
    — and the demon fox lay dead....
Yet there was never a sign of wound, and
    never a drop he bled.

"So that was the end of the great black fox,
    and here is the prize I've won;
And now for a drink to cheer me up — I've
    mushed since the early sun;
We'll drink a toast to the sorry ghost of the
    fox whose race is run."

## 2

Now Claw-fingered Kitty and Windy Ike, bad
    as the worst were they;
In their road-house down by the river-trail
    they waited and watched for prey;
With wine and song they joyed night long, and
    they slept like swine by day.

For things were done in the Midnight Sun
    that no tongue will ever tell;
And men there be who walk earth-free, but
    whose names are writ in hell —
Are writ in flames with the guilty names of
    Fournier and Labelle.

Put not your trust in a poke of dust would ye
    sleep the sleep of sin;
For there be those who would rob your clothes
    ere yet the dawn comes in;
And a prize likewise in a woman's eyes is a
    peerless black fox skin.

Put your faith in the mountain cat if you lie
    within his lair,
Trust the fangs of the mother-wolf, and the
    claws of the lead-ripped bear;
But oh, of the wiles and the gold-tooth smiles
    of a dance-hall wench beware!

## THE BALLAD OF THE BLACK FOX SKIN

Wherefore it was beyond all laws that lusts of
    man restrain,
A man drank deep and sank to sleep never to
    wake again;
And the Yukon swallowed through a hole the
    cold corpse of the slain.

## 3

The black fox skin a shadow cast from the
    roof nigh to the floor;
And sleek it seemed and soft it gleamed, and
    the woman stroked it o'er;
And the man stood by with a brooding eye,
    and gnashed his teeth and swore.

When thieves and thugs fall out and fight
    there's fell arrears to pay;
And soon or late sin meets its fate, and so it
    fell one day
That Claw-fingered Kitty and Windy Ike
    fanged up like dogs at bay.

"The skin is mine, all mine," she cried; "I did
    the deed alone."
"It's share and share with a guilt-yoked pair,"
    he hissed in a pregnant tone;
And so they snarled like malamutes over a
    mildewed bone.

## THE BALLAD OF THE BLACK FOX SKIN

And so they fought, by fear untaught, till
  haply it befell
One dawn of day she slipped away to Dawson
  town to sell
The fruit of sin, this black fox skin that had
  made their lives a hell.

She slipped away as still he lay, she clutched
  the wondrous fur;
Her pulses beat, her foot was fleet, her fear
  was as a spur;
She laughed with glee, she did not see him rise
  and follow her.

The bluffs uprear and grimly peer far over
  Dawson town;
They see its lights a blaze o' nights and harshly
  they look down;
They mock the plan and plot of man with
  grim, ironic frown.

The trail was steep; 'twas at the time when
  swiftly sinks the snow;
All honey-combed, the river ice was rotting
  down below;
The river chafed beneath its rind with many a
  mighty throe.

And up the swift and oozy drift a woman
    climbed in fear,
Clutching to her a black fox fur as if she held
    it dear;
And hard she pressed it to her breast — then
    Windy Ike drew near.

She made no moan — her heart was stone —
    she read his smiling face,
And like a dream flashed all her life's dark
    horror and disgrace;
A moment only — with a snarl he hurled her
    into space.

She rolled for nigh an hundred feet; she
    bounded like a ball;
From crag to crag she caromed down through
    snow and timber fall; . . .
A hole gaped in the river ice; the spray flashed
    — that was all.

A bird sang for the joy of spring, so piercing
    sweet and frail;
And blinding bright the land was dight in gay
    and glittering mail;
And with a wondrous black fox skin a man slid
    down the trail.

### 4

A wedge-faced man there was who ran along
    the river bank,
Who stumbled through each drift and slough,
    and ever slipped and sank,
And ever cursed his Maker's name, and ever
    "hooch" he drank.

He travelled like a hunted thing, hard harried,
    sore distrest;
The old grandmother moon crept out from
    her cloud-quilted nest;
The aged mountains mocked at him in their
    primeval rest.

Grim shadows diapered the snow; the air was
    strangely mild;
The valley's girth was dumb with mirth, the
    laughter of the wild;
The still sardonic laughter of an ogre o'er a
    child.

The river writhed beneath the ice; it groaned
    like one in pain,
And yawning chasms opened wide, and closed
    and yawned again;
And sheets of silver heaved on high until they
    split in twain.

## THE BALLAD OF THE BLACK FOX SKIN

From out the road-house by the trail they saw
   a man afar
Make for the narrow river-reach where the
   swift cross-currents are;
Where, frail and worn, the ice is torn and the
   angry waters jar.

But they did not see him crash and sink into
   the icy flow;
They did not see him clinging there, gripped
   by the undertow,
Clawing with bleeding finger-nails at the
   jagged ice and snow.

They found a note beside the hole where he
   had stumbled in:
"Here met his fate by evil luck a man who
   lived in sin,
And to the one who loves me least I leave this
   black fox skin."

And strange it is; for, though they searched
   the river all around,
No trace or sign of black fox skin was ever
   after found;
Though one man said he saw the tread of
   *hoofs* deep in the ground.

# The Prospector

I strolled up old Bonanza, where I staked in
　　ninety-eight,
　A-purpose to revisit the old claim.
I kept thinking mighty sadly of the funny
　　ways of Fate,
　And the lads who once were with me in the game.
Poor boys, they're down-and-outers, and there's scarcely one to-day
　Can show a dozen colors in his poke;
And me, I'm still prospecting, old and battered, gaunt and gray,
　And I'm looking for a grub-stake, and I'm broke.

I strolled up old Bonanza. The same old moon looked down;
　The same old landmarks seemed to yearn to me;
But the cabins all were silent, and the flat, once like a town,
　Was mighty still and lonesome-like to see.
There were piles and piles of tailings where we toiled with pick and pan,
　And turning round a bend I heard a roar,
And there a giant gold-ship of the very newest plan
　Was tearing chunks of pay-dirt from the shore.

It wallowed in its water-bed, it burrowed, heaved and swung;
　It gnawed its way ahead with grunts and sighs;
Its bill of fare was rock and sand; the tailings were its dung;
　It glared around with fierce electric eyes.
Full fifty buckets crammed its maw; it bellowed out for more;
　It looked like some great monster in the gloom.
With two to feed its sateless greed, it worked for seven score,
　And I sighed: "Ah, old-time miner, here's your doom!"

## THE PROSPECTOR

The idle windlass turns to rust; the sagging sluice-box falls;
    The holes you digged are water to the brim;
Your little sod-roofed cabins with the snugly moss-chinked walls
    Are deathly now and mouldering and dim.
The battle-field is silent where of old you fought it out;
    The claims you fiercely won are lost and sold.
But there's a little army that they'll never put to rout —
    The men who simply live to seek the gold.

The men who can't remember when they learned to swing a pack,
    Or in what lawless land the quest began;
The solitary seeker with his grub-stake on his back,
    The restless buccaneer of pick and pan.
On the mesas of the Southland, on the tundras of the North,
    You will find us, changed in face but still the same;
And it isn't need, it isn't greed that sends us faring forth —
    It's the fever, it's the glory of the game.

For once you've panned the speckled sand and seen the bonny dust,
    Its peerless brightness blinds you like a spell;
It's little else you care about; you go because you must,
    And you feel that you could follow it to hell.
You'd follow it in hunger, and you'd follow it in cold;
    You'd follow it in solitude and pain;
And when you're stiff and battened down let someone whisper "Gold,"
    You're lief to rise and follow it again.

Yet look you, if I find the stuff it's just like so much dirt;
    I fling it to the four winds like a child.
It's wine and painted women and the things that do me hurt,
    Till I crawl back, beggared, broken, to the Wild.

## THE PROSPECTOR

Till I crawl back, sapped and sodden, to my grub-stake and my tent —
　　There's a city, there's an army (hear them shout).
There's the gold in millions, millions, but I haven't got a cent;
　　And oh, it's me, it's me that found it out.

It was my dream that made it good, my dream that made me go
　　To lands of dread and death disprized of man;
But oh, I've known a glory that their hearts will never know,
　　When I picked the first big nugget from my pan.
It's still my dream, my dauntless dream, that drives me forth once more
　　To seek and starve and suffer in the Vast;
That heaps my heart with eager hope, that glimmers on before —
　　My dream that will uplift me to the last.

Perhaps I am stark crazy, but there's none of you too sane;
　　It's just a little matter of degree.
My hobby is to hunt out gold; it's fortressed in my brain;
　　It's life and love and wife and home to me.
And I'll strike it, yes, I'll strike it; I've a hunch I cannot fail;
　　I've a vision, I've a prompting, I've a call;
I hear the hoarse stampeding of an army on my trail,
　　To the last, the greatest gold camp of them all.

Beyond the shark-tooth ranges sawing savage at the sky
　　There's a lowering land no white man ever struck;
There's gold, there's gold in millions, and I'll find it if I die,
　　And I'm going there once more to try my luck.
Maybe I'll fail — what matter? It's a mandate, it's a vow;
　　And when in lands of dreariness and dread
You seek the last lone frontier, far beyond your frontiers now,
　　You will find the old prospector, silent, dead.

## THE PROSPECTOR

*You will find a tattered tent-pole with a ragged robe below it;*
  *You will find a rusted gold-pan on the sod;*
*You will find the claim I'm seeking, with my bones as stakes to show it;*
  *But I've sought the last Recorder, and He's — God.*

# The Rhyme of the Restless Ones

We couldn't sit and study for the law;
The stagnation of a bank we couldn't stand;
For our riot blood was surging, and we didn't
    need much urging
To excitements and excesses that are banned.
    So we took to wine and drink and other things,
  And the devil in us struggled to be free;
Till our friends rose up in wrath, and they pointed out the path,
  And they paid our debts and packed us o'er the sea.

Oh, they shook us off and shipped us o'er the foam,
To the larger lands that lure a man to roam;
  And we took the chance they gave
  Of a far and foreign grave,
And we bade good-by for evermore to home.

And some of us are climbing on the peak,
  And some of us are camping on the plain;
By pine and palm you'll find us, with never claim to bind us,
  By track and trail you'll meet us once again.

We are fated serfs to freedom — sky and sea;
  We have failed where slummy cities overflow;
But the stranger ways of earth know our pride and know our worth,
  And we go into the dark as fighters go.

## THE RHYME OF THE RESTLESS ONES

Yes, we go into the night as brave men go,
Though our faces they be often streaked with woe;
   Yet we're hard as cats to kill,
   And our hearts are reckless still,
And we've danced with death a dozen times or so.

And you'll find us in Alaska after gold,
   And you'll find us herding cattle in the South.
We like strong drink and fun, and, when the race is run,
   We often die with curses in our mouth.
We are wild as colts unbroke, but never mean.
   Of our sins we've shoulders broad to bear the blame;
But we'll never stay in town and we'll never settle down,
   And we'll never have an object or an aim.

No, there's that in us that time can never tame;
And life will always seem a careless game;
   And they'd better far forget —
   Those who say they love us yet —
Forget, blot out with bitterness our name.

# The Law of the Yukon

his is the law of the
Yukon, and ever
she makes it plain:
"Send not your foolish
and feeble; send me your
strong and your sane —
Strong for the red rage of battle; sane, for I
harry them sore;
Send me men girt for the combat, men who
are grit to the core;
Swift as the panther in triumph, fierce as the
bear in defeat,
Sired of a bulldog parent, steeled in the
furnace heat.
Send me the best of your breeding, lend me
your chosen ones;
Them will I take to my bosom, them will I call
my sons;
Them will I gild with my treasure, them will I
glut with my meat;
But the others — the misfits, the failures — I
trample under my feet.
Dissolute, damned and despairful, crippled and
palsied and slain,
Ye would send me the spawn of your gutters
— Go! take back your spawn again.

"Wild and wide are my borders, stern as death
is my sway;
From my ruthless throne I have ruled alone
for a million years and a day;

Hugging my mighty treasure, waiting for man
    to come,
Till he swept like a turbid torrent, and after
    him swept — the scum.
The pallid pimp of the dead-line, the enervate
    of the pen,
One by one I weeded them out, for all that I
    sought was — Men.
One by one I dismayed them, frighting them
    sore with my glooms;
One by one I betrayed them unto my manifold
    dooms.
Drowned them like rats in my rivers, starved
    them like curs on my plains,
Rotted the flesh that was left them, poisoned
    the blood in their veins;
Burst with my winter upon them, searing
    forever their sight,
Lashed them with fungus-white faces,
    whimpering wild in the night;

"Staggering blind through the storm-whirl,
    stumbling mad through the snow,
Frozen stiff in the ice-pack, brittle and bent
    like a bow;
Featureless, formless, forsaken, scented by
    wolves in their flight,
Left for the wind to make music through ribs
    that are glittering white;
Gnawing the black crust of failure, searching
    the pit of despair,
Crooking the toe in the trigger, trying to
    patter a prayer;

## THE LAW OF THE YUKON

Going outside with an escort, raving with lips
   all afoam,
Writing a cheque for a million, driveling
   feebly of home;
Lost like a louse in the burning ... or else in
   the tented town
Seeking a drunkard's solace, sinking and
   sinking down;
Steeped in the slime at the bottom, dead to a
   decent world,
Lost 'mid the human flotsam, far on the
   frontier hurled;
In the camp at the bend of the river, with its
   dozen saloons aglare,
Its gambling dens ariot, its gramophones all
   ablare;
Crimped with the crimes of a city, sin-ridden
   and bridled with lies,
In the hush of my mountained vastness, in the
   flush of my midnight skies.
Plague-spots, yet tools of my purpose, so
   natheless I suffer them thrive,
Crushing my Weak in their clutches, that only
   my Strong may survive.

"But the others, the men of my mettle, the
   men who would 'stablish my fame
Unto its ultimate issue, winning me honor, not
   shame;
Searching my uttermost valleys, fighting each
   step as they go,
Shooting the wrath of my rapids, scaling my
   ramparts of snow;

## THE LAW OF THE YUKON

Ripping the guts of my mountains, looting the
    beds of my creeks,
Them will I take to my bosom, and speak as a
    mother speaks.
I am the land that listens, I am the land that
    broods;
Steeped in eternal beauty, crystalline waters
    and woods.
Long have I waited lonely, shunned as a thing
    accurst,
Monstrous, moody, pathetic, the last of the
    lands and the first;
Visioning camp-fires at twilight, sad with a
    longing forlorn,
Feeling my womb o'er-pregnant with the seed
    of cities unborn.
Wild and wide are my borders, stern as death
    is my sway,
And I wait for the men who will win me —
    and I will not be won in a day;
And I will not be won by weaklings, subtle,
    suave and mild,
But by men with the hearts of vikings, and the
    simple faith of a child;
Desperate, strong and resistless, unthrottled by
    fear or defeat,
Them will I gild with my treasure, them will I
    glut with my meat.

"Lofty I stand from each sister land, patient
    and wearily wise,
With the weight of a world of sadness in my
    quiet, passionless eyes;
Dreaming alone of a people, dreaming alone of
    a day,

## THE LAW OF THE YUKON

When men shall not rape my riches, and curse
    me and go away;
Making a bawd of my bounty, fouling the hand
    that gave —
Till I rise in my wrath and I sweep on their
    path and I stamp them into a grave.
Dreaming of men who will bless me, of women
    esteeming me good,
Of children born in my borders of radiant
    motherhood,
Of cities leaping to stature, of fame like a flag
    unfurled,
As I pour the tide of my riches in the eager lap
    of the world."

This is the Law of the Yukon, that only the
    Strong shall thrive;
That surely the Weak shall perish, and only
    the Fit survive.
Dissolute, damned and despairful, crippled and
    palsied and slain,
This is the Will of the Yukon, — Lo, how she
    makes it plain!

# To the Man of the High North

y rhymes are rough, and
often in my rhyming
I've drifted, silver-sailed,
on seas of dream,
Hearing afar the bells of
Elfland chiming,
Seeing the groves of Arcadie agleam.

I was the thrall of Beauty that rejoices
    From peak snow-diademed to regal star;
Yet to mine aerie ever pierced the voices,
    The pregnant voices of the Things That Are.

The Here, the Now, the vast Forlorn around us;
    The gold-delirium, the ferine strife;
The lusts that lure us on, the hates that hound us;
    Our red rags in the patch-work quilt of Life.

The nameless men who nameless rivers travel,
    And in strange valleys greet strange deaths alone;
The grim, intrepid ones who would unravel
    The mysteries that shroud the Polar Zone.

These will I sing, and if one of you linger
    Over my pages in the Long, Long Night,
And on some lone line lay a calloused finger,
    Saying: "It's human-true — it hits me right";
Then will I count this loving toil well spent;
Then will I dream awhile — content, content.

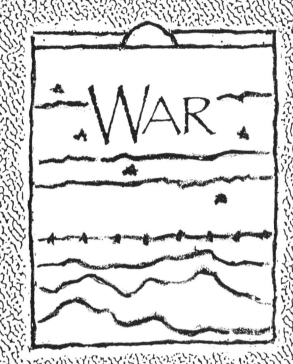

# Bill the Bomber

he poppies gleamed like bloody pools
  through cotton-woolly mist;
The Captain kept a-lookin' at the
  watch upon his wrist;
And there we smoked and squatted,
  as we watched the shrapnel flame;
'Twas wonnerful, I'm tellin' you, how fast them bullets came.
'Twas weary work the waiting, though; I tried to sleep a wink,
For waitin' means a-thinkin', and it doesn't do to think.
So I closed my eyes a little, and I had a niceish dream
Of a-standin' by a dresser with a dish of Devon cream;
But I hadn't time to sample it, for suddenlike I woke:
"Come on, me lads!" the Captain says, 'n I climbed out through
  the smoke.

We spread out in the open: it was like a bath of lead;
But the boys they cheered and hollered fit to raise the bloody dead,
Till a beastly bullet copped 'em, then they lay without a sound,
And it's odd — we didn't seem to heed them corpses on the ground.
And I kept on thinkin', thinkin', as the bullets faster flew,
How they picks the werry best men, and they lets the rotters through;
So indiscriminatin' like, they spares a man of sin,
And a rare lad wot's a husband and a father gets done in.
And while havin' these reflections and advancin' on the run,
A bullet biffs me shoulder, and says I: "That's number one."

Well, it downed me for a jiffy, but I didn't lose me calm,
For I knew that I was needed: I'm a bomber, so I am
I 'ad lost me cap and rifle, but I "carried on" because
I 'ad me bombs and knew that they was needed, so they was.

## BILL THE BOMBER

We didn't 'ave no singin' now, nor many men to cheer;
Maybe the shrapnel drowned 'em, crashin' out so werry near;
And the Maxims got us sideways, and the bullets faster flew,
And I copped one on me flipper, and says I: "That's number two."

I was pleased it was the left one, for I 'ad me bombs, ye see.
And 'twas 'ard if they'd be wasted like, and all along o' me.
And I'd lost me 'at and rifle — but I told you that before,
So I packed me mit inside me coat and "carried on" once more.
But the rumpus it was wicked, and the men were scarcer yet,
And I felt me ginger goin', but me jaws I kindo set,
And we passed the Boche first trenches, which was 'eapin' 'igh with dead,
And we started for their second, which was fifty feet ahead;
When something like a 'ammer smashed me savage on the knee,
And down I came all muck and blood: Says I: "That's number three."

So there I lay all 'elpless like, and bloody sick at that,
And worryin' like anythink, because I'd lost me 'at;
And thinkin' of me missis, and the partin' words she said:
"If you gets killed, write quick, ol' man, and tell me as you're dead."
And looking' at me bunch o' bombs — that was the 'ardest blow,
To think I'd never 'ave the chance to 'url them at the foe.
And there was all our boys in front, a-fightin' there like mad,
And me as could 'ave 'elped 'em wiv the lovely bombs I 'ad.
And so I cussed and cussed, and then I struggled back again,
Into that bit of battered trench, packed solid with its slain.

Now as I lay a-lyin' there and blastin' of me lot,
And wishin' I could just dispose of all them bombs I'd got,
I sees within the doorway of a shy, retirin' dug-out
Six Boches all a-grinnin', and their Captain stuck 'is mug out;
And they 'ad a nice machine gun, and I twigged what they was at;
And they fixed it on a tripod, and I watched 'em like a cat;

## BILL THE BOMBER

And they got it in position, and they seemed so werry glad,
Like they'd got us in a death-trap, which, condemn their souls! they 'ad.
For there our boys was fightin' fifty yards in front, and 'ere
This lousy bunch of Boches they 'ad got us in the rear.

Oh, it set me blood a-boilin' and I quite forgot me pain,
So I started crawlin', crawlin' over all them mounds of slain;
And them barstards was so busy-like they 'ad no eyes for me,
And me bleeding' leg was draggin', but me right arm it was free....
And now they 'ave it all in shape, and swingin' sweet and clear;
And now they're all excited like, but — I am drawin' near;
And now they 'ave it loaded up, and now they're takin' aim....
*Rat-tat-tat-tat!* Oh, here, says I, is where I join the game.
And my right arm it goes swingin', and a bomb it goes a-slingin',
And that "typewriter" goes wingin' in a thunderbolt of flame.

Then these Boches, wot was left of 'em, they tumbled down their 'ole,
And up I climbed a mound of dead, and down on them I stole.
And, oh, that blessed moment when I heard their frightened yell,
And I laughed down in that dug-out, ere I bombed their souls to hell.
And now I'm in the hospital, surprised that I'm alive;
We started out a thousand men, we came back thirty-five.
And I'm minus of a trotter, but I'm most amazin' gay,
For me bombs they wasn't wasted, though, you might say, "thrown away."

# The Revelation

he same old sprint in the
morning, boys, to the
same old din and smut;
Chained all day to the
same old desk, down
in the same old rut;
Posting the same old greasy books, catching the
same old train:
Oh, how will I manage to stick it all, if I ever get
back again?

We've bidden good-bye to life in a cage, we're
finished with pushing a pen;
They're pumping us full of bellicose rage,
they're showing us how to be men.
We're only beginning to find ourselves; we're
wonders of brawn and thew;
But when we go back to our Sissy jobs, — oh,
what are we going to do?

For shoulders curved with the counter stoop
will be carried erect and square;
And faces white from the office light will be
bronzed by the open air;
And we'll walk with the stride of a new-born
pride, with a new-found joy in our eyes,
Scornful men who have diced with death
under the naked skies.

## THE REVELATION

And when we get back to the dreary grind,
   and the bald-headed boss's call,
Don't you think that the dingy window-blind,
   and the dingier office wall,
Will suddenly melt to a vision of space, of
   violent, flame-scarred night?
Then ... oh, the joy of the danger-thrill, and
   oh, the roar of the fight!

Don't you think as we peddle a card of pins
   the counter will fade away,
And again we'll be seeing the sand-bag rims,
   and the barb-wire's misty grey?
As a flat voice asks for a pound of tea, don't
   you fancy we'll hear instead
The night-wind moan and the soothing drone
   of the packet that's overhead?

Don't you guess that the things we're seeing
   now will haunt us through all the years;
Heaven and hell rolled into one, glory and
   blood and tears;
Life's pattern picked with a scarlet thread,
   where once we wove with a grey
To remind us all how we played our part in the
   shock of an epic day?

Oh, we're booked for the Great Adventure
   now, we're pledged to the Real Romance;
We'll find ourselves or we'll lose ourselves
   somewhere in giddy old France;

## THE REVELATION

We'll know the zest of the fighter's life; the
  best that we have we'll give;
We'll hunger and thirst; we'll die ... but first
  — we'll live; by the gods, we'll live!

We'll breathe free air and we'll bivouac under
  the starry sky;
We'll march with men and we'll fight with
  men, and we'll see men laugh and die;
We'll know such joy as we never dreamed;
  we'll fathom the deeps of pain:
But the hardest bit of it all will be — when we
  come back home again.

*For some of us smirk in a chiffon shop, and some*
  *of us teach in a school;*
*Some of us help with the seat of our pants to*
  *polish an office stool;*
*The merits of somebody's soap or jam some of us*
  *seek to explain,*
*But all of us wonder what we'll do when we have*
  *to go back again.*

# Funk

When your marrer bone
 seems 'oller,
And you're glad you
 ain't no taller,
And you're all a-shakin'
 like you 'ad the chills;
When your skin creeps like a pullet's,
And you're duckin' all the bullets,
And you're green as gorgonzola round the gills;
When your legs seem made of jelly,
And you're squeamish in the belly,
And you want to turn about and do a bunk:
For Gawd's sake, kid, don't show it!
Don't let your mateys know it —
You're just sufferin' from funk, funk, funk.

Of course there's no denyin'
That it ain't so easy tryin'
To grin and grip your rifle by the butt,
When the 'ole world rips asunder,
And you sees yer pal go under,
As a bunch of shrapnel sprays 'im on the nut;
I admit it's 'ard contrivin'
When you 'ears the shells arrivin',
To discover you're a bloomin' bit o' spunk;
But, my lad, you've got to do it,
And your God will see you through it,
For wot 'E 'ates is funk, funk, funk.

## FUNK

So stand up, son; look gritty,
And just 'um a lively ditty,
And only be afraid to be afraid;
Just 'old yer rifle steady,
And 'ave yer bay'nit ready,
For that's the way good soldier-men is made.
And if you 'as to die,
As it sometimes 'appens, why,
Far better die a 'ero than a skunk;
A-doin' of yer bit,
And so — to 'ell with it,
There ain't no bloomin' funk, funk, funk.

# Normandy Peasant

hey've taken all my
    fields of corn
To make them strips
    of strife;
They've razed the house
    where I was born
And lived in all my life.
Where once I jolted with content
    Along deep rutted lanes,
They've straddled runways of cement
    To ground their aeroplanes.

They've made me sell my bit of land
    And paid me with their gold.
Alas, they could not understand
    It was my heart I sold.
From my beloved soil bereft
    It was my soul I gave,
And now I know there's nothing left
    Between me and the grave.

They say that progress must go on
    Though darkly glooms the Pit.
Ah well, my life is nearly gone
    And I am glad of it.
Then buy my land and millions spend
    To sponsor war's red woe,
And what will be the awful end
    Thank God! I'll never know.

## NORMANDY PEASANT

For oh the world is in a mess,
 And day by day grows worse;
I've had my bid of happiness
 And now I know the Curse
Of monstrous might and speed that's blind,
 And see, as fails my breath,
The doom of martyred humankind,
 When Science mates with Death.

# The Haggis of Private McPhee

ae ye heard whit ma auld
    mither's postit tae me?
It fair maks me hamesick,"
    says Private McPhee.
"And whit did she send ye?"
    says Private McPhun,
As he cockit his rifle and bleezed at a Hun.
"A haggis! A *Haggis!*" says Private McPhee;
"The brawest big haggis I ever did see.
And think! it's the morn when fond memory turns
Tae haggis and whuskey — the Birthday o' Burns.
We maun find a dram; then we'll ca' in the rest
O' the lads, and we'll hae a Burns' Nicht wi' the best."

"Be ready at sundoon," snapped Sergeant McCole;
"I want you two men for the List'nin' Patrol."
Then Private McPhee looked at Private McPhun:
"I'm thinkin', ma lad, we're confoundedly done."
Then Private McPhun looked at Private McPhee:
"I'm thinkin' auld chap, it's a' aff wi' oor spree."
But up spoke their crony, wee Wullie McNair:
"Jist lea' yer braw haggis for me tae prepare;
And as for the dram, if I search the camp roun',
We maun hae a drappie tae jist haud it doon.
Sae rin, lads, and think, though the nicht it be black,
O' the haggis that's waiting' ye when ye get back."

My! but it wis waesome on Naebuddy's Land,
And the deid they were rottin' on every hand.
And the rockets like corpse candles hauntit the sky,
And the winds o' destruction went shudderin' by.

## THE HAGGIS OF PRIVATE McPHEE

There wis skelpin' o' bullets and skirlin' o' shells,
And breengin' o' bombs and a thoosand death-knells;
But cooryin' doon in a Jack Johnson hole
Little fashed the twa men o' the List'nin' Patrol.
For sweeter than honey and bricht as a gem
Wis the thocht o' the haggis that waitit for them.

Yet alas! in oor moments o' sunniest cheer
Calamity's aften maist cruelly near.
And while the twa talked o' their puddin' divine
The Boches below them were howkin' a mine.
And while the twa cracked o' the feast they would hae,
The fuse it wis burnin' and burnin' away.
Then sudden a roar like the thunner o' doom,
A hell-leap o' flame ... then the wheesht o' the tomb.

"Haw, Jock! Are ye hurtit?" says Private McPhun.
"Ay, Geordie, they've got me; I'm fearin' I'm done.
It's ma leg; I'm jist thinkin' it's aff at the knee;
Ye'd best gang and leave me," says Private McPhee.
"Oh leave ye I wunna," says Private McPhun;
"And leave ye I canna, for though I micht run,
It's no faur I wud gang, it's no muckle I'd see:
I'm blindit, and that's whit's the maitter wi' me."
Then Private McPhee sadly shakit his heid:
"If we bide here for lang, we'll be bidin' for deid.
And yet, Geordie lad, I could gang weel content
If I'd tasted that haggis ma auld mither sent."
"That's droll," says McPhun; "ye've jist speakit ma mind.
Oh I ken it's a terrible thing tae be blind;
And yet it's no that that embitters ma lot—
It's missin' that braw muckle haggis ye've got."
For a while they were silent; then up once again
Spoke Private McPhee, though he whussilt wi' pain:

## THE HAGGIS OF PRIVATE McPHEE

"And why should we miss it? Between you and me
We've legs for tae run, and we've eyes for tae see.
You lend me your shanks and I'll lend you ma sicht,
And we'll baith hae a kyte-fu' o' haggis the nicht."

Oh the sky it wis dourlike and dreepin' a wee,
When Private McPhun gruppit Private McPhee.
Oh the glaur it wis fylin' and crieshin' the grun',
When Private McPhee guidit Private McPhun.
"Keep clear o' them corpses — they're maybe no deid!
Haud on! There's a big muckle crater aheid.
Look oot! There's a sap; we'll be haein' a coup.
A staur-shell! For Godsake! Doun, lad, on yer daup.
Bear aff tae yer richt.... Aw yer jist daein' fine:
Before the nicht's feenished on haggis we'll dine."

There wis death and destruction on every hand;
There wis havoc and horror on Naebuddy's Land.
And the shells bickered doun wi' a crump and a glare,
And the hameless wee bullets were dingin' the air.
Yet on they went staggerin', cooryin' doun
When the stutter and cluck o' a Maxim crept roun'.
And the legs o' McPhun they were sturdy and stoot,
And McPhee on his back kept a bonnie look-oot.
"On, on, ma brave lad! We're no faur frae the goal;
I can hear the braw sweerin' o' Sergeant McCole."

But strength has its leemit, and Private McPhun,
Wi' a sab and a curse fell his length on the grun'.
Then Private McPhee shoutit doon in his ear:
"Jist think o' the haggis! I smell it from here.
It's gushin' wi' juice, it's embaumin' the air;
It's steamin' for us, and we're — jist — aboot — there."

## THE HAGGIS OF PRIVATE McPHEE

Then Private McPhun answers: "Dommit, auld chap!
For the sake o' that haggis I'll gang till I drap."
And he gets on his feet wi' a heave and a strain,
And onward he staggers in passion and pain.
And the flare and the glare and the fury increase,
Till you'd think they'd jist taken a' hell on a lease.
And on they go reelin' in peetifu' plight,
And someone is shoutin' away on their right;
And someone is runnin', and noo they can hear
A sound like a prayer and a sound like a cheer;
And swift through the crash and the flash and the din,
The lads o' the Hielands are bringin' them in.

"They're baith sairly woundit, but is it no droll
Hoo they rave aboot haggis?" says Sergeant McCole.
When hirplin alang comes wee Wullie McNair,
And they a' wonnert why he wis greetin' sae sair.
And he says: "I'd jist liftit it oot o' the pot,
And there it lay steamin' and savoury hot,
When sudden I dooked at the fleech o' a shell,
And it — *drapped on the haggis and dinged it tae hell.*"

And oh but the lads were fair taken aback;
Then sudden the order wis passed tae attack,
And up from the trenches like lions they leapt,
And on through the nicht like a torrent they swept.
On, on, wi' their bayonets thirstin' before!
On, on tae the foe wi' a rush and a roar!
And wild to the welkin their battle-cry rang,
And doon on the Boches like tigers they sprang:
And there wisna a man but had death in his ee,
For he thocht o' the haggis o' Private McPhee.

# Wounded

**I**s it not strange?
 A year ago to-day,
With scarce a thought
 beyond the hum-
 drum round,
I did my decent job and
 earned my pay;
Was averagely happy, I'll be bound.
Ay, in my little groove I was content,
Seeing my life run smoothly to the end,
With prosy days in stolid labour spent,
And jolly nights, a pipe, a glass, a friend.
In God's good time a hearth fire's cosy gleam,
A wife and kids, and all a fellow needs;
When presto! like a bubble goes my dream:
I leap upon the Stage of Splendid Deeds.
I yell with rage; I wallow deep in gore:
I, that was clerk in a drysalter's store.

Stranger than any book I've ever read.
Here on the reeking battlefield I lie,
Under the stars, propped up with smeary dead,
Like too, if no one takes me in, to die.
Hit on the arms, legs, liver, lungs and gall;
Damn glad there's nothing more of me to hit;
But calm, and feeling never pain at all,
And full of wonder at the turn of it.
For of the dead around me three are mine,
Three foemen vanquished in the whirl of fight;
So if I die I have no right to whine,
I feel I've done my little bit all right.

WOUNDED

I don't know how — but there the beggars are,
As dead as herrings pickled in a jar.

And here am I, worse wounded than I thought;
For in the fight a bullet bee-like stings;
You never heed; the air is metal-hot,
And all alive with little flicking wings.
*But on you charge.* You see the fellows fall;
Your pal was by your side, fair fighting-mad;
You turn to him, and lo! no pal at all;
You wonder vaguely if he's copped it bad.
*But on you charge.* The heavens vomit death;
And vicious death is besoming the ground.
You're blind with sweat; you're dazed, and out of breath,
And though you yell, you cannot hear a sound.
*But on you charge.* Oh, War's a rousing game!
Around you smoky clouds like ogres tower;
The earth is rowelled deep with spurs of flame,
And on your helmet stones and ashes shower.
*But on you charge.* It's odd! You have no fear.
Machine-gun bullets whip and lash your path;
Red, yellow, black and smoky giants rear;
The shrapnel rips, the heavens roar in wrath.
*But on you charge.* Barbed wire all trampled down.
The ground all gored and rent as by a blast;
Grim heaps of grey where once were heaps of brown;
A ragged ditch — the Hun first line at last.
All smashed to hell. Their second right ahead,
*So on you charge.* There's nothing else to do.
More reeking holes, blood, barbed wire, gruesome dead;
(Your puttee strap's undone — that worries you).
You glare around. You think you're all alone.
But no; your chums come surging left and right.
The nearest chap flops down without a groan,
His face still snarling with the rage of fight.

## WOUNDED

Ha! here's the second trench — just like the first,
Only a little more so, more "laid out";
More pounded, flame-corroded, death-accurst;
A pretty piece of work, beyond a doubt.
Now for the third, and there your job is done,
*So on you charge.* You never stop to think.
Your cursed puttee's trailing as you run;
You feel you'd sell your soul to have a drink.
The acrid air is full of cracking whips.
You wonder how it is you're going still.
You foam with rage. Oh, God! to be at grips
With someone you can rush and crush and kill.
Your sleeve is dripping blood; you're seeing red;
You're battle-mad; your turn is coming now.
See! there's the jagged barbed wire straight ahead,
And there's the trench — you'll get there anyhow.
Your puttee catches on a strand of wire,
And down you go; perhaps it saves your life,
For over sandbag rims you see 'em fire,
Crop-headed chaps, their eyes ablaze with strife.
You crawl, you cower; then once again you plunge
With all your comrades roaring at your heels.
*Have at 'em, lads!* You stab, you jab, you lunge;
A blaze of glory, then the red world reels.
A crash of triumph, then ... you're faint a bit ...
That cursed puttee! Now to fasten it....

Well, that's the charge. And now I'm here alone.
I've built a little wall of Hun on Hun,
To shield me from the leaden bees that drone
(It saves me worry, and it hurts 'em none).
The only thing I'm wondering is when
Some stretcher-men will stroll along my way?
It isn't much that's left of me, but then
Where life is, hope is, so at least they say.

## WOUNDED

Well, if I'm spared I'll be the happy lad.
I tell you I won't envy any king.
I've stood the racket, and I'm proud and glad;
I've had my crowning hour. Oh, War's the thing!
It gives us common, working chaps our chance,
A taste of glory, chivalry, romance.

Ay, War, they say, is hell; it's heaven, too.
It lets a man discover what he's worth.
It takes his measure, shows what he can do,
Gives him a joy like nothing else on earth.
It fans in him a flame that otherwise
Would flicker out, these drab, discordant days;
It teaches him in pain and sacrifice
Faith, fortitude, grim courage past all praise.
Yes, War is good. So here beside my slain,
A happy wreck I wait amid the din;
For even if I perish mine's the gain....
Hi, there, you fellows! *Won't* you take me in?
Give me a fag to smoke upon the way....
We've taken La Boiselle! The hell, you say!
Well, that would make a corpse sit up and grin....
Lead on! I'll live to fight another day.

# My Job

I've got a little job on 'and, the time is drawin' nigh;
  At seven by the Captain's watch I'm due to go and do it;
I wants to 'ave it nice and neat, and pleasin' to the eye,
And I 'opes the God of soldier men will see me safely through it.
Because, you see, it's somethin' I 'ave never done before;
And till you 'as experience noo stunts is always tryin';
The chances is I'll never 'ave to do it any more:
At seven by the Captain's watch my little job is . . . *dyin'*.

I've got a little note to write; I'd best begin it now.
I ain't much good at writin' notes, but here goes: "Dearest Mother,
I've been in many 'ot old 'do's'; I've scraped through safe some'ow,
But now I'm on the very point of tacklin' another.
A little job of hand-grenades; they called for volunteers.
They picked me out; I'm proud of it; it seems a trifle dicky.
If anythin' should 'appen, well, there ain't no call for tears,
And so . . . I 'opes this finds you well. — Your werry lovin' Micky."

I've got a little score to settle wiv them swine out there.
I've 'ad so many of me pals done in it's quite upset me.
I've seen so much of bloody death I don't seem for to care,
If I can only even up, how soon the blighters get me.
I'm sorry for them perishers that corpses in a bed;
I only 'opes mine's short and sweet, no linger-longer-lyin';
I've made a mess of life, but now I'll try to make instead . . .
It's seven sharp. Good-bye, old pals! . . . *a decent job in dyin'*.

# The Black Dudeen

*Humping it here in*
*the dug-out,*
*Sucking me black*
*dudeen,*
*I'd like to say in*
*a general way,*
*There's nothing like Nickyteen;*
*There's nothing like Nickyteen, me boys,*
*Be it pipes or snipes or cigars;*
*So be sure that a bloke*
*Has plenty to smoke,*
*If you wants him to fight your wars.*

When I've eat my fill and my belt is snug,
I begin to think of my baccy plug.
I whittle a fill in my horny palm,
And the bowl of me old clay pipe I cram.
I trim the edges, I tamp it down,
I nurse a light with an anxious frown;
I begin to draw, and my cheeks tuck in,
And all my face is a blissful grin;
And up in a cloud the good smoke goes,
And the good pipe glimmers and fades and glows;
In its throat it chuckles a cheery song,
For I likes it hot and I likes it strong.
Oh, it's good is grub when you're feeling hollow,
But the best of a meal's the smoke to follow.

## THE BLACK DUDEEN

There was Micky and me on a night patrol,
Having to hide in a fizz-bang hole;
And sure I thought I was worse than dead
Wi' them crump-crumps hustlin' over me head.
Sure I thought 'twas the dirty spot,
Hammer and tongs till the air was hot.
And mind you, water up to your knees.
And cold! A monkey of brass would freeze.
And if we ventured our noses out
A "typewriter" clattered its pills about.
The field of glory! Well, I don't think!
I'd sooner be safe and snug in clink.

Then Micky, he goes and he cops one bad,
He always was having ill-luck, poor lad.
Says he: "Old chummy, I'm booked right through;
Death and me 'as a wrongday voo.
But . . . 'aven't you got a pinch of shag? —
I'd sell me perishin' soul for a fag."
And there he shivered and cussed his luck,
So I gave him me old black pipe to suck.
And he heaves a sigh, and he takes to it
Like a babby takes to his mammy's tit;
Like an infant takes to his mother's breast,
Poor little Micky! he went to rest.

But the dawn was near, though the night was black,
So I left him there and I started back.
And I laughed as the silly old bullets came,
For the bullet ain't made wot's got me name.
Yet some of 'em buzzed onhealthily near,
And one little blighter just chipped me ear.

## THE BLACK DUDEEN

But there! I got to the trench all right,
When sudden I jumped wi' a start o' fright,
And a word that doesn't look well in type:
*I'd clean forgotten me old clay pipe.*

So I had to do it all over again,
Crawling out on that filthy plain.
Through shells and bombs and bullets and all —
Only this time — I do not crawl.
I run like a man wot's missing a train,
Or a tom-cat caught in a plump of rain.
I hear the spit of a quick-fire gun
Tickle my heels, but I run, I run.
Through crash and crackle, and flicker and flame,
(Oh, the packet ain't issued wot's got me name!)
I run like a man that's no ideer
Of hunting around for a sooveneer.
I run bang into a German chap,
And he stares like an owl, so I bash his map.
And just to show him that I'm his boss,
I gives him a kick on the parados.
And I marches him back with me all serene,
With, *tucked in me gub, me old dudeen.*

*Sitting here in the trenches*
*Me heart's a-splittin' with spleen,*
*For a parcel o' lead comes missing me head,*
*But it smashes me old dudeen.*
*God blast that red-headed sniper!*
*I'll give him somethin' to snipe;*
*Before the war's through*
*Just see how I do*
*That blighter that smashed me pipe.*

# The Odyssey of 'Erbert 'Iggins

Me and Ed
   and a
   stretcher
Out on the
   nootral
   ground.
(If there's one dead corpse, I'll betcher
There's a 'undred smellin' around.)
Me and Eddie O'Brian,
Both of the R.A.M.C.
"It's a 'ell of a night
For a soul to take flight,"
As Eddie remarks to me.
Me and Ed crawlin' 'omeward,
Thinkin' our job is done,
When sudden and clear,
Wot do we 'ear:
'Owl of a wounded 'Un.

"Got to take 'im," snaps Eddie;
"Got to take all we can.
'E may be a Germ
Wiv the 'eart of a worm,
But, blarst 'im! ain't 'e a man?"
So 'e sloshes out fixin' a dressin'
('E'd always a medical knack),
When that wounded 'Un
'E rolls to 'is gun,
And 'e plugs me pal in the back.

## THE ODYSSEY OF 'ERBERT 'IGGINS

Now what would you do? I arst you.
There was me slaughtered mate.
There was that 'Un
(I'd collered 'is gun),
A-snarlin' 'is 'ymn of 'ate.
Wot did I do? 'Ere, whisper . . .
'E'd a shiny bald top to 'is 'ead,
But when I got through,
Between me and you,
It was 'orrid and jaggy and red.

" 'Ang on like a limpet, Eddie.
Thank Gord! you ain't dead after all."
It's slow and it's sure and it's steady
(Which is 'ard, for 'e's big and I'm small).
The rockets are shootin' and shinin',
It's rainin' a perishin' flood,
The bullets are buzzin' and whinin',
And I'm up to me stern in the mud.
There's all kinds of 'owlin' and 'ootin';
It's black as a bucket of tar;
Oh, I'm doin' my bit,
But I'm 'avin' a fit,
And I wish I was 'ome wiv Mar.

"Stick on like a plaster, Eddie.
Old sport, you're a-slackin' your grip."
Gord! But I'm crocky already;
My feet, 'ow they slither and slip!
There goes the biff of a bullet.
The Boches have got us for fair.
Another one — *Whut!*
The son of a slut!

## THE ODYSSEY OF 'ERBERT 'IGGINS

'E managed to miss by a 'air.
'Ow! Wot was it jabbed at me shoulder?
Gave it a dooce of a wrench.
Is it Eddie or me
Wot's a-bleedin' so free?
Crust! but it's long to the trench.
I ain't just as strong as a Sandow,
And Ed ain't a flapper by far;
I'm blamed if I understand 'ow
We've managed to get where we are.
But 'ere's for a bit of a breather.
"Steady there, Ed, 'arf a mo'.
Old pal, it's all right;
It's a 'ell of a fight,
But are we down-'earted? No-o-o."
Now war is a funny thing, ain't it?
It's the rummiest sort of a go.
For when it's most real,
It's then that you feel
You're a-watchin' a cinema show.
'Ere's me wot's a barber's assistant.
Hey, presto! It's somewheres in France,
And I'm 'ere in a pit
Where a coal-box 'as 'it,
And it's all like a giddy romance.
The ruddy quick-firers are spittin',
The 'eavies are bellowin' 'ate,
And 'ere I am cashooly sittin',
And 'oldin' the 'ead of me mate.
Them gharstly green star-shells is beamin',
'Ot shrapnel is poppin' like rain,
And I'm sayin': "Bert 'Iggins, you're dreamin',
And you'll wake up in 'Ampstead again.
You'll wake up and 'ear yourself sayin':
'Would you like, sir, to 'ave a shampoo?'

## THE ODYSSEY OF 'ERBERT 'IGGINS

'Stead of sheddin' yer blood
In the rain and the mud,
Which is some'ow the right thing to do;
Which is some'ow yer 'oary-eyed dooty,
Wot you're doin' the best wot you can,
For 'Ampstead and 'ome and beauty,
And you've been and you've slaughtered a man.
A feller wot punctured your partner;
Oh, you 'ammered 'im 'ard on the 'ead,
And you still see 'is eyes
Starin' bang at the skies,
And you ain't even sorry 'e's dead.
But you wish you was back in your diggin's
Asleep on your mouldy old stror.
Oh, you're doin' yer bit, 'Erbert 'Iggins,
But you ain't just enjoyin' the war."

" 'Ang on like a hoctopus, Eddie.
It's us for the bomb-belt again.
Except for the shrap
Which 'as 'it me a tap,
I'm feelin' as right as the rain.
It's my silly old feet wot are slippin',
It's as dark as a 'ogs'ead o' sin,
But don't be oneasy, my pippin,
I'm goin' to pilot you in.
It's my silly old 'ead wot is reelin'.
The bullets is buzzin' like bees.
Me shoulder's red-'ot,
And I'm bleedin' a lot,
And me legs is on'inged at the knees.
But we're staggerin' nearer and nearer.
Just stick it, old sport, play the game.
I make 'em out clearer and clearer,
Our trenches a-snappin' with flame.

## THE ODYSSEY OF 'ERBERT 'IGGINS

Oh, we're stumblin' closer and closer.
'Ang on there, lad! Just one more try.
Did you say: Put you down? Damn it, no, sir!
I'll carry you in if I die.
By cracky! old feller, they've seen us.
They're sendin' out stretchers for two.
Let's give 'em the hoorah between us
('Anged lucky we aren't booked through).
My flipper is mashed to a jelly.
A bullet 'as tickled your spleen.
We've shed lots of gore
And we're leakin' some more,
But — wot a hoccasion it's been!
Ho! 'Ere comes the rescuin' party.
They're crawlin' out cautious and slow.
Come! Buck up and greet 'em, my 'earty,
Shoulder to shoulder — so.
They mustn't think we was down-'earted.
Old pal, we was never down-'earted.
If they arsts us if we was down-'earted
We'll 'owl in their fyces: 'No-o-o!' "

# A Song of Winter Weather

It isn't the foe that
we fear;
It isn't the bullets
that whine;
It isn't the
business career
Of a shell, or the bust of a mine;
It isn't the snipers who seek
To nip our young hopes in the bud:
No, it isn't the guns,
And it isn't the Huns —
It's the *mud*,

     *mud*,

          *mud*.

It isn't the *mêlée* we mind.
That often is rather good fun.
It isn't the shrapnel we find
Obtrusive when rained by the ton;
It isn't the bounce of the bombs
That gives us a positive pain:
It's the strafing we get
When the weather is wet —
It's the *rain*,

     *rain*,

          *rain*.

## A SONG OF WINTER WEATHER

It isn't because we lack grit
We shrink from the horrors of war.
We don't mind the battle a bit;
In fact that is what we are for;
It isn't the rum-jars and things
Make us wish we were back in the fold:
It's the fingers that freeze
In the boreal breeze —
It's the *cold*,
        *cold*,
           *cold*.

Oh, the rain, the mud, and the cold,
The cold, the mud, and the rain;
With weather at zero it's hard for a hero
From language that's rude to refrain.
With porridgy muck to the knees,
With sky that's a-pouring a flood,
Sure the worst of our foes
Are the pains and the woes
Of the *rain*,
        the *cold*,
           and the *mud*.

# The Ballad of Soulful Sam

ou want me to tell you a story, a yarn of
    the firin' line,
Of our thin red kharki 'eroes, out there
    where the bullets whine;
Out there where the bombs are bustin', and
    the cannons like 'ell-doors slam —
Just order another drink, boys, and I'll tell you of Soulful Sam.

Oh, Sam, he was never 'ilarious, though I've 'ad some mates as was wus;
He 'adn't C. B. on his programme, he never was known to cuss.
For a card or a skirt or a beer-mug he 'adn't a friendly word;
But when it came down to Scriptures, say! Wasn't he just a bird!

He always 'ad tracts in his pocket, the which he would haste to present,
And though the fellers would use them in ways that they never was meant,
I used to read 'em religious, and frequent I've been impressed
By some of them bundles of 'oly dope he carried around in his vest.

For I — and oh, 'ow I shudder at the 'orror the word conveys!
'Ave been — let me whisper it 'oarsely — a gambler 'alf of me days;
A gambler, you 'ear — a gambler. It makes me wishful to weep,
And yet 'ow it's true, my brethren! — I'd rather gamble than sleep.

I've gambled the 'ole world over, from Monte Carlo to Maine;
From Dawson City to Dover, from San Francisco to Spain.
Cards! They 'ave been me ruin. They've taken me pride and me pelf,
And when I'd no one to play with — why, I'd go and I'd play by meself.

## THE BALLAD OF SOULFUL SAM

And Sam 'e would sit and watch me, as I shuffled a greasy deck,
And 'e'd say: "You're bound to Perdition," And I'd answer: "Git off me neck!"
And that's 'ow we came to get friendly, though built on a different plan,
Me wot's a desprite gambler, 'im sich a good young man.

But on to me tale. Just imagine ... Darkness! The battle-front!
The furious 'Uns attackin'! Us ones a-bearin' the brunt!
Me crouchin' be'ind a sandbag, trying' 'ard to keep calm,
When I 'ears someone singin' a 'ymn toon; be'old! it is Soulful Sam.

Yes; right in the crash of the combat, in the fury of flash and flame,
'E was shootin' and singin' serenely as if 'e enjoyed the same.
And there in the 'eat of the battle, as the 'ordes of demons attacked,
He dipped down into 'is tunic, and 'e 'anded me out a tract.

Then a star-shell flared, and I read it: Oh, Flee From the Wrath to Come!
Nice cheerful subject, I tell yer, when you're 'earin' the bullets 'um.
And before I 'ad time to thank 'im, just one of them bits of lead
Comes slingin' along in a 'urry, and it 'its my partner.... Dead?

No, siree! not by a long sight! For it plugged 'im 'ard on the chest,
Just where 'e'd tracts for a army corps stowed away in 'is vest.
On its mission of death that bullet 'ustled along, and it caved
A 'ole in them tracts to 'is 'ide, boys — but the life o' me pal was saved.

And there as 'e showed me in triumph, and 'orror was chokin' me breath,
On came another bullet on its 'orrible mission of death;
On through the night it cavorted, seekin' its 'aven of rest,
And it zipped through a crack in the sandbags, and it walloped me bang
    on the breast.

## THE BALLAD OF SOULFUL SAM

Was I killed, do you ask? Oh no, boys. Why am I sittin' 'ere
Gazin' with mournful vision at a mug long empty of beer?
With a throat as dry as a — oh, thanky! I don't much mind if I do.
Beer with a dash of 'ollands, that's my particular brew.

Yes, that was a terrible moment. It 'ammered me 'ard o'er the 'eart;
It bowled me down like a nine-pin, and I looked for the gore to start;
And I saw in the flash of a moment, in that thunder of hate and strife,
Me wretched past like a pitchur — the sins of a gambler's life.

For I 'ad no tracts to save me, to thwart that mad missile's doom;
I 'ad no pious pamphlets to 'elp me to cheat the tomb;
I 'ad no 'oly leaflets to baffle a bullet's aim;
I'd only — a deck of cards, boys, but ... *it seemed to do just the same.*

# A Song of the Sandbags

O, Bill, I'm not a-spooning out no
    patriotic tosh
(The cove be'ind the sandbags ain't
    a death-or-glory cuss).
And though I strafes 'em good and
    'ard I doesn't 'ate the Boche,
I guess they're mostly decent, just the same as most of us.
I guess they loves their 'omes and kids as much as you or me;
And just the same as you or me they'd rather shake than fight;
And if we'd 'appened to be born at Berlin-on-the-Spree,
We'd be out there with 'Ans and Fritz, dead sure that we was right.

    A-standin' up to the sandbags
    It's funny the thoughts wot come;
    Starin' into the darkness,
    'Earin' the bullets 'um;
    (Zing! Zip! Ping! Rip!
    'Ark 'ow the bullets 'um!)
    A-leanin' against the sandbags
    Wiv me rifle under me ear,
    Oh, I've 'ad more thoughts on a sentry-go
    Than I used to 'ave in a year.

I wonder, Bill, if 'Ans and Fritz is wonderin' like me
Wot's at the bottom of it all? Wot all the slaughter's for?
'E thinks 'e's right (of course 'e ain't) but this we both agree,
If them as made it 'ad to fight, there wouldn't be no war.
If them as lies in feather beds while we kips in the mud;
If them as makes their fortoons while we fights for 'em like 'ell;
If them as slings their pot of ink just 'ad to sling their blood:
By Crust! I'm thinkin' there 'ud be another tale to tell.

A SONG OF THE SANDBAGS

Shiverin' up to the sandbags,
With a hicicle 'stead of a spine,
Don't it seem funny the things you think
'Ere in the firin' line:
(Whee! Whut! Ziz! Zut!
Lord! 'Ow the bullets whine!)
Hunkerin' down when a star-shell
Cracks in a sputter of light,
You can jaw to yer soul by the sandbags
Most any old time o' night.

They talks o' England's glory and a-'oldin' of our trade,
Of Empire and 'igh destiny until we're fair flim-flammed;
But if it's for the likes o' that that bloody war is made,
Then wot I say is: Empire and 'igh destiny be damned!
There's only one good cause, Bill, for poor blokes like us to fight:
That's self-defence, for 'earth and 'ome, and them that bears our name;
And that's wot I'm a-doin' by the sandbags 'ere to-night....
But Fritz out there will tell you 'e's a-doin' of the same.

Starin' over the sandbags,
Sick of the 'ole damn thing;
Firin' to keep meself awake,
'Earin' the bullets sing.
(Hiss! Twang! Tsing! Pang!
Saucy the bullets sing.)
Dreamin' 'ere by the sandbags
Of a day when war will cease,
When 'Ans and Fritz and Bill and me
Will clink our mugs in fraternity,
And the Brotherhood of Labour will be
The Brotherhood of Peace.

# Young Fellow My Lad

"here are you going,
    Young Fellow My Lad,
On this glittering morn
    of May?"
"I'm going to join the
    Colours, Dad;
They're looking for men, they say."
"But you're only a boy, Young Fellow My Lad;
You aren't obliged to go."
"I'm seventeen and a quarter, Dad,
And ever so strong, you know."

"So you're off to France, Young Fellow My Lad,
And you're looking so fit and bright."
"I'm terribly sorry to leave you, Dad,
But I feel that I'm doing right."
"God bless you and keep you, Young Fellow My Lad,
You're all of my life, you know."
"Don't worry. I'll soon be back, dear Dad,
And I'm awfully proud to go."

"Why don't you write, Young Fellow My Lad?
I watch for the post each day;
And I miss you so, and I'm awfully sad,
And it's months since you went away.
And I've had the fire in the parlour lit,
And I'm keeping it burning bright
Till my boy comes home; and here I sit
Into the quiet night."

## YOUNG FELLOW MY LAD

"What is the matter, Young Fellow My Lad?
No letter again to-day.
Why did the postman look so sad,
And sigh as he turned away?
I hear them tell that we've gained new ground,
But a terrible price we've paid:
God grant, my boy, that you're safe and sound;
But oh I'm afraid, afraid."

"They've told me the truth, Young Fellow My Lad:
You'll never come back again:
(Oh God! the dreams and the dreams I've had,
And the hopes I've nursed in vain!)
For you passed in the night, Young Fellow My Lad,
And you proved in the cruel test
Of the screaming shell and the battle hell
That my boy was one of the best.

"So you'll live, you'll live, Young Fellow My Lad,
In the gleam of the evening star,
In the wood-note wild and the laugh of the child,
In all sweet things that are.
And you'll never die, my wonderful boy,
While life is noble and true;
For all our beauty and hope and joy
We will owe to our lads like you."

# Going Home

'm goin' 'ome to Blighty —
    ain't I glad to 'ave the chance!
I'm loaded up wiv fightin',
    and I've 'ad my fill o' France;
I'm feelin' so excited-like,
    I want to sing and dance,
For I'm goin' 'ome to Blighty in the mawnin'.

I'm goin' 'ome to Blighty: can you wonder as I'm gay?
I've got a wound I wouldn't sell for 'alf a year o' pay;
A harm that's mashed to jelly in the nicest sort o' way,
    For it takes me 'ome to Blighty in the mawnin'.

'Ow everlastin' keen I was on gettin' to the front!
I'd ginger for a dozen, and I 'elped to bear the brunt;
But Cheese and Crust! I'm crazy, now I've done me little stunt,
    To sniff the air of Blighty in the mawnin'.

I've looked upon the wine that's white, and on the wine that's red;
I've looked on cider flowin', till it fairly turned me 'ead;
But oh, the finest scoff will be, when all is done and said,
    A pint o' Bass in Blighty in the mawnin'.

I'm goin' back to Blighty, which I left to strafe the 'Un;
I've fought in bloody battles, and I've 'ad a 'eap of fun;
But now me flipper's busted, and I think me dooty's done,
    And I'll kiss me gel in Blighty in the mawnin'.

## GOING HOME

Oh, there be furrin lands to see, and some of 'em be fine;
And there be furrin gels to kiss, and scented furrin wine;
But there's no land like England, and no other gel like mine:
    Thank Gawd for dear old Blighty in the mawnin'.

# Afternoon Tea

s I was saying ... (No, thank you; I never take cream with my tea; Cows weren't allowed in the trenches — got out of the habit, y'see.)
As I was saying, our Colonel leaped up like a
    youngster of ten:
"Come on, lads!" he shouts, "and we'll show 'em."
    And he sprang to the head of the men.
Then some bally thing seemed to trip him, and
    he fell on his face with a slam....
Oh, he died like a true British soldier, and the
    last word he uttered was "Damn!"
And hang it! I loved the old fellow, and
    something just burst in my brain,
And I cared no more for the bullets than I
    would for a shower of rain.
'Twas an awf'ly funny sensation (I say, this is
    jolly nice tea);
I felt as if something had broken; by gad! I was
    suddenly free.
Free for a glorified moment, beyond
    regulations and laws,
Free just to wallow in slaughter, as the chap of
    the Stone Age was.
So on I went joyously nursing a Berserker rage
    of my own,
And though all my chaps were behind me,
    feeling most frightf'ly alone;
With the bullets and shells ding-donging, and
    the "krock" and the swish of the shrap;

## AFTERNOON TEA

And I found myself humming "Ben Bolt" . . .
   (Will you pass me the sugar, old chap?
Two lumps, please). . . . What was I saying?
   Oh yes, the jolly old dash;
We simply ripped through the barrage, and on
   with a roar and a crash.
My fellows — Old Nick couldn't stop 'em. On,
   on they went with a yell,
Till they tripped on the Boches' sand-bags, —
   nothing much left to tell:
A trench so tattered and battered that even a
   rat couldn't live;
Some corpses tangled and mangled, wire you
   could pass through a sieve.
The jolly old guns had bilked us, cheated us
   out of our show,
And my fellows were simply yearning for a red
   mix-up with the foe.
So I shouted to them to follow, and on we
   went roaring again,
Battle-tuned and exultant, on in the leaden
   rain.
Then all at once a machine gun barks from a
   bit of a bank,
And our Major roars in a fury: "We've got to
   take it on flank."
He was running like fire to lead us, when
   down like a stone he comes,
As full of "typewriter" bullets as a pudding is
   full of plums.
So I took his job and we got 'em. . . . By gad!
   we got 'em like rats;
Down in a deep shell-crater we fought like
   Kilkenny cats.

## AFTERNOON TEA

'Twas pleasant just for a moment to be
    sheltered and out of range,
With someone you *saw* to go for — it made an
    agreeable change.
And the Boches that missed my bullets, my
    chaps gave a bayonet jolt,
And all the time, I remember, I whistled and
    hummed "Ben Bolt."

Well, that little job was over, so hell for
    leather we ran,
On to the second line trenches, — that's
    where the fun began.
For though we had strafed 'em like fury, there
    still were some Boches about,
And my fellows, teeth set and eyes glaring, like
    terriers routed 'em out.
Then I stumbled on one of their dug-outs, and
    I shouted: "Is anyone there?"
And a voice, "Yes, one; but I'm wounded,"
    came faint up the narrow stair;
And my man was descending before me, when
    sudden a cry! a shot!
(I say, this cake is delicious. You make it
    yourself, do you not?)
My man? Oh, they killed the poor devil; for if
    there was one there was ten;
So after I'd bombed 'em sufficient I went
    down at the head of my men,
And four tried to sneak from a bunk-hole, but
    we cornered the rotters all right;
I'd rather not go into details, 'twas messy that
    bit of the fight.
But all of it's beastly messy; let's talk of
    pleasanter things:

## AFTERNOON TEA

The skirts that the girls are wearing, ridiculous
   fluffy things,
So short that they show.... Oh, hang it!
   Well, if I must, I must.
We cleaned out the second trench line, bomb
   and bayonet thrust;
And on we went to the third one, quite
   calloused to crumping by now;
And some of our fellows who'd passed us were
   making a deuce of a row;
And my chaps — well, I just couldn't hold
   'em; (It's strange how it is with gore;
In some ways it's just like whiskey: if you taste
   it you must have more.)
Their eyes were like beacons of battle; by gad,
   sir! they *couldn't* be calmed,
So I headed 'em bang for the bomb-belt,
   racing like billy-be-damned.
Oh, it didn't take long to arrive there, those
   who arrived at all;
The machine guns were certainly chronic, the
   shindy enough to appal.
Oh yes, I omitted to tell you, I'd wounds on
   the chest and the head,
And my shirt was torn to a gun-rag, and my
   face blood-gummy and red.
I'm thinking I looked like a madman; I fancy I
   felt one too,
Half naked and swinging a rifle.... God! what
   a glorious "do."
As I sit here in old Piccadilly, sipping my
   afternoon tea,
I see a blind, bullet-chipped devil, and it's hard
   to believe that it's me;
I see a wild, war-damaged demon, smashing
   out left and right,

And humming "Ben Bolt" rather loudly, and
    hugely enjoying the fight.
And as for my men, may God bless 'em! I've
    loved 'em ever since then:
They fought like the shining angels; they're
    the pick o' the land, my men.
And the trench was a reeking shambles, not a
    Boche to be seen alive —
So I thought; but on rounding a traverse I
    came on a covey of five;
And four of 'em threw up their flippers, but
    the fifth chap, a sergeant, was game,
And though I'd a bomb and revolver he came
    at me just the same.
A sporty thing that, I tell you; I just couldn't
    blow him to hell,
So I swung to the point of his jaw-bone, and
    down like a nine-pin he fell.
And then when I'd brought him to reason, he
    wasn't half bad, that Hun;
He bandaged my head and my short-rib as well
    as the Doc could have done.
So back I went with my Boches, as gay as a
    two-year-old colt,
And it suddenly struck me as rummy, I still
    was a-humming "Ben Bolt."
And now, by Jove! how I've bored you. You've
    just let me babble away;
Let's talk of the things that *matter* — your
    car or the newest play....

# The March of the Dead

The cruel war was over —
    oh, the triumph was so sweet!
We watched the troops returning,
    through our tears;
There was triumph, triumph, triumph
    down the scarlet glittering street,
  And you scarce could hear the music for the cheers.
And you scarce could see the house-tops for the flags that flew between;
  The bells were pealing madly to the sky;
And everyone was shouting for the Soldiers of the Queen,
  And the glory of an age was passing by.

And then there came a shadow, swift and sudden, dark and drear;
  The bells were silent, not an echo stirred.
The flags were drooping sullenly, the men forgot to cheer;
  We waited, and we never spoke a word.
The sky grew darker, darker, till from out the gloomy rack
  There came a voice that checked the heart with dread:
"Tear down, tear down your bunting now, and hang up sable black;
  They are coming — it's the Army of the Dead."

They were coming, they were coming, gaunt and ghastly, sad and slow;
  They were coming, all the crimson wrecks of pride;
With faces seared, and cheeks red smeared, and haunting eyes of woe,
  And clotted holes the khaki couldn't hide.
Oh, the clammy brow of anguish! the livid, foam-flecked lips!
  The reeling ranks of ruin swept along!
The limb that trailed, the hand that failed, the bloody finger tips!
  And oh, the dreary rhythm of their song!

### THE MARCH OF THE DEAD

"They left us on the veldt-side, but we felt we couldn't stop
    On this, our England's crowning festal day;
We're the men of Magersfontein, we're the men of Spion Kop,
    Colenso — we're the men who had to pay.
We're the men who paid the blood-price. Shall the grave be all our gain?
    You owe us. Long and heavy is the score.
Then cheer us for our glory now, and cheer us for our pain,
    And cheer us as ye never cheered before."

The folks were white and stricken, and each tongue seemed weighted with lead;
    Each heart was clutched in hollow hand of ice;
And every eye was staring at the horror of the dead,
    The pity of the men who paid the price.
They were come, were come to mock us, in the first flush of our peace;
    Through writhing lips their teeth were all agleam;
They were coming in their thousands — oh, would they never cease!
    I closed my eyes, and then — it was a dream.

There was triumph, triumph, triumph down the scarlet gleaming street;
    The town was mad; a man was like a boy.
A thousand flags were flaming where the sky and city meet;
    A thousand bells were thundering the joy.
There was music, mirth and sunshine; but some eyes shone with regret;
    And while we stun with cheers our homing braves,
O God, in Thy great mercy, let us nevermore forget
    The graves they left behind, the bitter graves.

# The Bohemian

U p in my garret bleak
    and bare
I tilted back on my
    broken chair,
And my three old pals
    were with me there,
  Hunger and Thirst and Cold;
Hunger scowled at his scurvy mate:
Cold cowered down by the hollow grate,
And I hated them with a deadly hate
  As old as life is old.

So up in my garret that's near the sky
I smiled a smile that was thin and dry:
"You've roomed with me twenty year," said I,
  "Hunger and Thirst and Cold;
But now, begone down the broken stair!
I've suffered enough of your spite ... so there!"
Bang! Bang! I slapped on the table bare
  A glittering heap of gold.

"Red flames will jewel my wine to-night;
I'll loose my belt that you've lugged so tight;
Ha! Ha! Dame Fortune is smiling bright;
  The stuff of my brain I've sold;
*Canaille* of the gutter, up! Away!
You've battened on me for a bitter-long day;
But I'm driving you forth, and forever and aye,
  Hunger and Thirst and Cold."

## THE BOHEMIAN

So I kicked them out with a scornful roar;
Yet, oh, they turned at the garret door;
Quietly there they spoke once more:
    "The tale is not all told.
It's *au revoir*, but it's not good-by;
We're yours, old chap, till the day you die;
Laugh on, you fool! Oh, you'll never defy
    Hunger and Thirst and Cold."

# L'Escargot D'Or

O Tavern of the
   Golden Snail!
Ten *sous* have I,
   so I'll regale;
Ten *sous* your amber
   brew to sip
(Eight for the *bock* and two the tip),
And so I'll sit the evening long,
And smoke my pipe and watch the throng,
The giddy crowd that drains and drinks,
I'll watch it quiet as a sphinx;
And who among them all shall buy
For ten poor *sous* such joy as I?
As I who, snugly tucked away,
Look on it all as on a play,
A frolic scene of love and fun,
To please an audience of One.

O Tavern of the Golden Snail!
You've stuff indeed for many a tale.
All eyes, all ears, I nothing miss:
Two lovers lean to clasp and kiss;
The merry students sing and shout,
The nimble *garçons* dart about;
Lo! here come Mimi and Musette
With: "*S'il vous plait, une cigarette?*"
Marcel and Rudolf, Schaunard too,
Behold the old rapscallion crew,
With flowing tie and shaggy head . . .
Who says Bohemia is dead?
Oh shades of Murger! prank and clown,
And I will watch and write it down.

## L'ESCARGOT D'OR

O Tavern of the Golden Snail!
What crackling throats have gulped your ale!
What sons of Fame from far and near
Have glowed and mellowed in your cheer!
Within this corner where I sit
Banville and Coppée clashed their wit;
And hither too, to dream and drain,
And drown despair, came poor Verlaine.
Here Wilde would talk and Synge would muse,
Maybe like me with just ten *sous*.
Ah! one is lucky, is one not?
With ghosts so rare to drain a pot!
So may your custom never fail,
O Tavern of the Golden Snail!

# Julot the Apache

ou've heard of Julot the *apache*, and
Gigolette, his *môme*....
Montmartre was their hunting-ground,
but Belville was their home.
A little chap just like a boy, with smudgy
black mustache, —
Yet there was nothing juvenile in Julot the *apache*.
From head to heel as tough as steel, as nimble as a cat,
With every trick of twist and kick, a master of *savate*.
And Gigolette was tall and fair, as stupid as a cow,
With three combs in the greasy hair she banged upon her brow.
You'd see her on the Place Pigalle on any afternoon,
A primitive and strapping wench as brazen as the moon.
And yet there is a tale that's told of Clichy after dark,
And two *gendarmes* who swung their arms with Julot for a mark.
And oh, but they'd have got him too; they banged and blazed away,
When like a flash a woman leapt between them and their prey.
She took the medicine meant for him; she came down with a crash ...
"Quick now, and make your get-away, O Julot the *apache!*"
But no! He turned, ran swiftly back, his arms around her met;
They nabbed him sobbing like a kid, and kissing Gigolette.

Now I'm a reckless painter chap who loves a jamboree,
And one night in Cyrano's bar I got upon a spree;
And there were trollops all about, and crooks of every kind,
But though the place was reeling round I didn't seem to mind.
Till down I sank, and all was blank when in the bleary dawn
I woke up in my studio to find — my money gone;
Three hundred francs I'd scraped and squeezed to pay my quarter's rent.
"Someone has pinched my wad," I wailed; "it never has been spent."
And as I racked my brains to seek how I could raise some more,
Before my cruel landlord kicked me cowering from the door:

## JULOT THE APACHE

A knock ... "Come in," I gruffly groaned; I did not raise my head,
Then lo! I heard a husky voice, a swift and silky tread:
"You got so blind, last night, *mon vieux*, I collared all your cash —
Three hundred francs.... There! *Nom de Dieu*," said Julot the *apache*.

And that was how I came to know Julot and Gigolette,
And we would talk and drink a *bock*, and smoke a cigarette.
And I would meditate upon the artistry of crime,
And he would tell of cracking cribs and cops and doing time;
Or else when he was flush of funds he'd carelessly explain
He'd biffed some bloated *bourgeois* on the border of the Seine.
So gentle and polite he was, just like a man of peace,
And not a desperado and the terror of the police.

Now one day in a *bistro* that's behind the Place Vendôme
I came on Julot the *apache*, and Gigolette his *môme*.
And as they looked so very grave, says I to them, says I,
"Come on and have a little glass, it's good to rinse the eye.
You both look mighty serious; you've something on the heart."
"Ah, yes," said Julot the *apache*, "we've something to impart.
When such things come to folks like us, it isn't very gay ...
It's Gigolette — she tells me that a *gosse* is on the way."
Then Gigolette, she looked at me with eyes like stones of gall:
"If we were honest folks," said she, "I wouldn't mind at all.
But then ... you know the life we lead; well, anyway I mean
(That is, providing it's a girl) to call her Angeline."
"Cheer up," said I; "it's all in life. There's gold within the dross.
Come on, we'll drink another *verre* to Angeline the *gosse*."

And so the weary winter passed, and then one April morn
The worthy Julot came at last to say the babe was born.
"I'd like to chuck it in the Seine," he sourly snarled, "and yet
I guess I'll have to let it live, because of Gigolette."

I only laughed, for sure I saw his spite was all a bluff,
And he was prouder than a prince behind his manner gruff.
Yet every day he'd blast the brat with curses deep and grim,
And swear to me that Gigolette no longer thought of *him*.
And then one night he dropped the mask; his eyes were sick with dread,
And when I offered him a smoke he groaned and shook his head:
"I'm all upset; it's Angeline ... she's covered with a rash ...
She'll maybe die, my little *gosse*," cried Julot the *apache*.

But Angeline, I joy to say, came through the test all right,
Though Julot, so they tell me, watched beside her day and night.
And when I saw him next, says he: "Come up and dine with me.
We'll buy a beefsteak on the way, a bottle and some *brie*."
And so I had a merry night within his humble home,
And laughed with Angeline the *gosse* and Gigolette the *môme*.
And every time that Julot used a word the least obscene,
How Gigolette would frown at him and point to Angeline:
Oh, such a little innocent, with hair of silken floss,
I do not wonder they were proud of Angeline the *gosse*.
And when her arms were round his neck, then Julot says to me:
"I must work harder now, *mon vieux*, since I've to work for three."
He worked so very hard indeed, the police dropped in one day,
And for a year behind the bars they put him safe away.

So dark and silent now, their home; they'd gone — I wondered where,
Till in a laundry near I saw a child with shining hair;
And o'er the tub a strapping wench, her arms in soapy foam;
Lo! it was Angeline the *gosse*, and Gigolette the *môme*.
And so I kept an eye on them and saw that all went right,
Until at last came Julot home, half crazy with delight.
And when he'd kissed them both, says he: "I've had my fill this time.
I'm on the honest now, I am; I'm all fed up with crime.
You mark my words, the page I turn is going to be clean,
I swear it on the head of her, my little Angeline."

## JULOT THE APACHE

And so, to finish up my tale, this morning as I strolled
Along the boulevard I heard a voice I knew of old.
I saw a rosy little man with walrus-like mustache ...
I stopped, I stared.... By all the gods! 'twas Julot the *apache*.
"I'm in the garden way," he said, "and doing mighty well;
I've half an acre under glass, and heaps of truck to sell.
Come out and see. Oh come, my friend, on Sunday, wet or shine ...
Say! — *it's the First Communion of that little girl of mine.*"

# The Absinthe Drinkers

He's yonder, on the terrace of the
    Café de la Paix,
The little wizened Spanish man,
    I see him every day.
He's sitting with his Pernod on his
    customary chair;
He's staring at the passers with his customary stare.
He never takes his piercing eyes from off that moving throng,
That current cosmopolitan meandering along:
Dark diplomats from Martinique, pale Rastas from Peru,
An Englishman from Bloomsbury, a Yank from Kalamazoo;
A poet from Montmartre's heights, a dapper little Jap,
Exotic citizens of all the countries on the map;

A tourist horde from every land that's underneath the sun —
That little wizened Spanish man, he misses never one.
Oh, foul or fair he's always there, and many a drink he buys,
And there's a fire of red desire within his hollow eyes.
And sipping of my Pernod, and a-knowing what I know,
Sometimes I want to shriek aloud and give away the show.
I've lost my nerve; he's haunting me; he's like a beast of prey,
That Spanish man that's watching at the Café de la Paix.

Say! Listen and I'll tell you all ... the day was growing dim,
And I was with my Pernod at the table next to him;
And he was sitting soberly as if he were asleep,
When suddenly he seemed to tense, like tiger for a leap.
And then he swung around to me, his hand went to his hip,
My heart was beating like a gong — my arm was in his grip;

# THE ABSINTHE DRINKERS

His eyes were glaring into mine; aye, though I shrank with fear,
His fetid breath was on my face, his voice was in my ear:
"Excuse my *brusquerie*," he hissed; "but, sir, do you suppose —
That portly man who passed us had a *wen upon his nose?*"

And then a last it dawned on me, the fellow must be mad;
And when I soothingly replied: "I do not think he had,"
The little wizened Spanish man subsided in his chair,
And shrouded in his raven cloak resumed his owlish stare.
But when I tried to slip away he turned and glared at me,
And oh, that fishlike face of his was sinister to see:
"Forgive me if I startled you; of course you think I'm queer;
No doubt you wonder who I am, so solitary here;
You question why the passers-by I piercingly review . . .
Well, listen, my bibacious friend, I'll tell my tale to you.

"It happened twenty years ago, and in another land:
A maiden young and beautiful, two suitors for her hand.
My rival was the lucky one; I vowed I would repay;
Revenge has mellowed in my heart, it's rotten ripe to-day.
My happy rival skipped away, vamoosed, he left no trace;
And so I'm waiting, waiting here to meet him face to face;
For has it not been ever said that all the world one day
Will pass in pilgrimage before the Café de la Paix?"

"But, sir," I made remonstrance, "if it's twenty years ago,
You'd scarcely recognize him now, he must have altered so."
The little wizened Spanish man he laughed a hideous laugh,
And from his cloak he quickly drew a faded photograph.
"You're right," said he, "but there are traits (oh, this you must allow)
That never change; Lopez was fat, he must be fatter now.

## THE ABSINTHE DRINKERS

His paunch is senatorial, he cannot see his toes,
I'm sure of it; and then, behold! that wen upon his nose.
I'm looking for a man like that. I'll wait and wait until ..."
"What will you do?" I sharply cried; he answered me: "Why, kill!
He robbed me of my happiness — nay, stranger, do not start;
I'll firmly and politely put — a bullet in his heart."

And then that little Spanish man, with big cigar alight,
Uprose and shook my trembling hand and vanished in the night.
And I went home and thought of him and had a dreadful dream
Of portly men with each a wen, and woke up with a scream.
And sure enough, next morning, as I prowled the Boulevard,
A portly man with wenny nose roamed into my regard;
Then like a flash I ran to him and clutched him by the arm:
"Oh, sir," said I, "I do not wish to see you come to harm;
But if your life you value aught, I beg, entreat and pray —
Don't pass before the terrace of the Café de la Paix."
That portly man he looked at me with such a startled air,
Then bolted like a rabbit down the rue Michaudière.
"Ha! ha! I've saved a life," I thought; and laughed in my relief,
And straightway joined the Spanish man o'er his *apéritif*.
And thus each day I dodged about and kept the strictest guard
For portly men with each a wen upon the Boulevard.
And then I hailed my Spanish pal, and sitting in the sun,
We ordered many Pernods and we drank them every one.
And sternly he would stare and stare until my hand would shake,
And grimly he would glare and glare until my heart would quake.
And I would say: "Alphonso, lad, I must expostulate;
Why keep alive for twenty years the furnace of your hate?
Perhaps his wedded life was hell; and you, at least, are free ..."
"That's where you've got it wrong," he snarled; "the fool she took was *me*.
My rival sneaked, threw up the sponge, betrayed himself a churl:
'Twas he who got the happiness, I only got — the girl."
With that he looked so devil-like he made me creep and shrink,
And there was nothing else to do but buy another drink.

## THE ABSINTHE DRINKERS

Now yonder like a blot of ink he sits across the way,
Upon the smiling terrace of the Café de la Paix;
That little wizened Spanish man, his face is ghastly white,
His eyes are staring, staring like a tiger's in the night.
I know within his evil heart the fires of hate are fanned,
I know his automatic's ready waiting to his hand.
I know a tragedy is near. I dread, I have no peace . . .
Oh, don't you think I ought to go and call upon the police?
Look there . . . he's rising up . . . my God! He leaps from out his place . . .
Yon millionaire from Argentine . . . the two are face to face . . .
A shot! A shriek! A heavy fall! A huddled heap! Oh, see
The little wizened Spanish man is dancing in his glee. . . .
I'm sick . . . I'm faint . . . I'm going mad . . . Oh, please take me away . . .
There's BLOOD upon the terrace of the Café de la Paix. . . .

# The Philistine and the Bohemian

She was a Philistine
    spick and span,
He was a bold Bohemian.
She had the *mode*, and
    the last at that;
He had a cape and a brigand hat.
She was so *riante* and *chic* and trim;
He was so shaggy, unkempt and grim.
On the rue de la Paix she was wont to shine;
The rue de la Gaîté was more his line.
She doted on Barclay and Dell and Caine;
He quoted Mallarmé and Paul Verlaine.
She was a triumph at Tango teas;
At Vorticist's suppers he sought to please.
She thought that Franz Lehar was utterly great;
Of Strauss and Stravinski he'd piously prate.
She loved elegance, he loved art;
They were as wide as the poles apart:
Yet — Cupid and Caprice are hand and glove —
They met at a dinner, they fell in love.

Home he went to his garret bare,
Thrilling with rapture, hope, despair.
Swift he gazed in his looking-glass,
Made a grimace and murmured: "Ass!"
Seized his scissors and fiercely sheared,
Severed his buccaneering beard;
Grabbed his hair, and clip! clip! clip!
Off came a bunch with every snip.
Ran to a tailor's in startled state,
Suits a dozen commanded straight;

## THE PHILISTINE AND THE BOHEMIAN

Coats and overcoats, pants in pairs,
Everything that a dandy wears;
Socks and collars, and shoes and ties,
Everything that a dandy buys.
Chums looked at him with wondering stare,
Fancied they'd seen him before somewhere;
A Brummell, a D'Orsay, a *beau* so fine,
A shining, immaculate Philistine.

Home she went in a raptured daze,
Looked in a mirror with startled gaze,
Didn't seem to be pleased at all;
Savagely muttered: "Insipid Doll!"
Clutched her hair and a pair of shears,
Cropped and bobbed it behind the ears;
Aimed at a wan and willowy-necked
Sort of a Holman Hunt effect;
Robed in subtile and sage-green tones,
Like the dames of Rossetti and E. Burne-Jones;
Girdled her garments billowing wide,
Moved with an undulating glide;
All her frivolous friends forsook,
Cultivated a soulful look;
Gushed in a voice with a creamy throb
Over some weirdly Futurist daub —
Did all, in short, that a woman can
To be a consummate Bohemian.

A year went past with its hopes and fears,
A year that seemed like a dozen years.
They met once more.... Oh, at last! At last!
They rushed together, they stopped aghast.
They looked at each other with blank dismay,
They simply hadn't a word to say.

## THE PHILISTINE AND THE BOHEMIAN

He thought with a shiver: "Can this be she?"
She thought with a shudder: "This can't be he?"
This simpering dandy, so sleek and spruce;
This languorous lily in garments loose;
They sought to brace from the awful shock:
Taking a seat, they tried to talk.
She spoke of Bergson and Pater's prose,
He prattled of dances and ragtime shows;
She purred of pictures, Matisse, Cezanne,
His tastes to the girls of Kirchner ran;
She raved of Tschaikowsky and Caesar Franck,
He owned that he was a jazz-band crank!
They made no headway. Alas! alas!
He thought her a bore, she thought him an ass.
And so they arose and hurriedly fled;
Perish Illusion, Romance, you're dead.
He loved elegance, she loved art,
Better at once to part, to part.

And what is the moral of all this rot?
Don't try to be what you know you're not.
And if you're made on a muttonish plan,
Don't seek to seem a Bohemian;
And if to the goats your feet incline,
Don't try to pass for a Philistine.

# Muguet

T was on the sacred
First of May
I made a
sentimental sally
To buy myself a
slender spray
Of pearly lily of the valley;
And setting it beside my bed,
Dream back the smile of one now dead.

But when I asked how much a spray?
The figure seemed so astronomic
I rather fear that my dismay
Must have appeared a little comic.
The price, the shopgirl gravely said,
Alas! was fifteen francs a head.

However, I said: "Give me three,
And wrap them in a silver paper,
And I will take them home with me,
And light an 'in memoriam' taper,
To one whose smile, so heaven bright,
Was wont to make my darkness light."

Then lo! I saw beside me stand
A woman shabby, old and grey,
Who pointed with a trembling hand
And shyly asked: "How much are they?"

But when I told her, sadly said:
"I'll save my francs for milk and bread.

"Yet I've a daughter just sixteen,
Long sick abed and oh so sad.
I thought — well, how they would have been
A gift, maybe, to make her glad ..."
And then I saw her eyes caress
My blossoms with such wistfulness.

*I gave them:* sought my garret bare,
Knowing that she whom I had loved
Although no blooms I brought her there,
Would have so tenderly approved ...
And in the dark I lay awhile,
Seeing again her radiant smile.

# Finistère

Hurrah! I'm off to Finistère,
    to Finistère, to Finistère;
My satchel's swinging on my back,
    my staff is in my hand;
I've twenty *louis* in my purse, I know
    the sun and sea are there,
And so I'm starting out to-day to tramp the golden land.
I'll go alone and glorying, with on my lips a song of joy;
I'll leave behind the city with its canker and its care;
I'll swing along so sturdily — oh, won't I be the happy boy!
A-singing on the rocky roads, the roads of Finistère.

Oh, have you been to Finistère, and do you know a whin-grey town
That echoes to the clatter of a thousand wooden shoes?
And have you seen the fisher-girls go gallivantin' up and down,
And watched the tawny boats go out, and heard the roaring crews?
Oh, would you sit with pipe and bowl, and dream upon some sunny quay,
Or would you walk the windy heath and drink the cooler air;
Oh, would you seek a cradled cove and tussle with the topaz sea! —
Pack up your kit to-morrow, lad, and haste to Finistère.

Oh, I will go to Finistère, there's nothing that can hold me back.
I'll laugh with Yves and Léon, and I'll chaff with Rose and Jeanne;
I'll seek the little, quaint *buvette* that's kept by Mother Merdrinac,
Who wears a cap of many frills, and swears just like a man.
I'll yarn with hearty, hairy chaps who dance and leap and crack their heels;
Who swallow cupfuls of cognac and never turn a hair;
I'll watch the nut-brown boats come in with mullet, plaice and conger eels,
The jewelled harvest of the sea they reap in Finistère.

## FINISTÈRE

Yes, I'll come back from Finistère with memories of shining days,
Of scaly nets and salty men in overalls of brown;
Of ancient women knitting as they watch the tethered cattle graze
By little nestling beaches where the gorse goes blazing down;
Of headlands silvering the sea, of Calvarys against the sky,
Of scorn of angry sunsets, and of Carnac grim and bare;
Oh, won't I have the leaping veins, and tawny cheek and sparkling eye,
When I come back to Montparnasse and dream of Finistère.

REFLECTIONS

# Fore-Warning

I'd rather be the Jester than
    the Minstrel of the King;
I'd rather jangle cap and bells
    than twang the stately harp;
I'd rather make His royal ribs
    with belly-laughter ring,
Than see him sitting in the suds and sulky as a carp.
I'd rather be the Court buffoon than its most high-browed sage:
    So you who read, take heed, take heed, —
    Ere yet you turn my page.

# I Believe

t's my belief
    that every man
Should do his
    share of work,
And in our
    economic plan
  No citizen should shirk.
That in return each one should get
  His meed of fold and food,
And feel that all his toil and sweat
  Is for the common good.

It's my belief that every chap
  Should have an equal start,
And there should be no handicap
  To hinder his depart;
That there be fairness in the fight,
  And justice in the race,
And every lad should have the right
  To win his proper place.

It's my belief that people should
  Be neither rich nor poor;
That none should suffer servitude,
  And all should be secure.
That wealth is loot, and rank is rot,
  And foul is class and clan;
That to succeed a man may not
  Exploit his brother man.

## I BELIEVE

It's my belief that heritage
    And usury are wrong;
That each should win a worthy wage
    And sing an honest song....
Not one like this — for though I rue
    The wrong of life, I flout it.
Alas! I'm not prepared to do
    A goddam thing about it.

# Dirt

irt is just matter
out of place,
So scientists aver;
But when I see a
miner's face
I wonder if they err.
For grit and grime and grease may be
In God's constructive plan,
A symbol of nobility,
The measure of a man.

There's nought so clean as honest dirt,
So of its worth I sing;
I value more an oily shirt
Than garment of a king.
There's nought so proud as honest sweat,
And though its stink we cuss,
We kid-glove chaps are in the debt
Of those who sweat for us.

It's dirt and sweat that makes us folks
Proud as we are today;
We owe our wealth to weary blokes
Befouled by soot and clay.
And where you see a belly fat
A dozen more are lean....
By God! I'd sooner doff my hat
To washer-wife than queen.

DIRT

So here's a song to dirt and sweat,
   A grace to grit and grime;
A hail to workers who beget
   The wonders of our time.
And as they gaze, though gutter-girt,
   To palaces enskied,
Let them believe, by sweat and dirt,
   They, too, are glorified.

# Resentment

 man's a mug to
　　slog away
And stint himself
　　of ease,
When bureaucrats
　　take half his pay
　To glut their treasuries.
A guy's a dope to work like hell
　To make one dollar two,
When most of it will go to swell
　The fiscal revenue.

So you who gripe at super-tax
　Of sixty-five per cent,
Why don't you blissfully relax,
　And beat the government?
Cut down to half the work you do,
　Contrive on less to live:
Go easy on the job and you
　Will have less gain to give.

Just plumb refuse to slave and sweat;
　Forbear to do your best,
When only half your wage you get
　And taxes claim the rest.
Although your talents go to rust,
　Your usefulness abate....
Why make an extra dollar just
　To give it to the State?

## RESENTMENT

If I possessed a million I
    Would change it all to gold,
And in a safe my bedside nigh
    My treasure I would hold.
And though a tenth each year I spent,
    I'd live in leisure lax
On capital — Oh! So content
    To bilk the income tax!

# The Song of the Wage-Slave

hen the long, long day is
over, and the Big Boss
gives me my pay,
I hope that it won't be hell-
fire, as some of the
parsons say.
And I hope that it won't be heaven, with some of
the parsons I've met —
All I want is just quiet, just to rest and forget.
Look at my face, toil-furrowed; look at my calloused
hands;
Master, I've done Thy bidding, wrought in Thy
many lands —
Wrought for the little masters, big-bellied they be,
and rich;
I've done their desire for a daily hire, and I die like
a dog in a ditch.
I have used the strength Thou hast given, Thou
knowest I did not shirk;
Threescore years of labor — Thine be the long day's
work.
And now, Big Master, I'm broken and bent and
twisted and scarred,
But I've held my job, and Thou knowest, and Thou
will not judge me hard.
Thou knowest my sins are many, and often I've
played the fool —
Whiskey and cards and women, they made me the
devil's tool.
I was just like a child with money; I flung it away
with a curse,
Feasting a fawning parasite, or glutting a harlot's
purse;

## THE SONG OF THE WAGE-SLAVE

Then back to the woods repentant, back to the mill
   or the mine,
I, the worker of workers, everything in my line.
Everything hard but headwork (I'd no more brains
   than a kid),
A brute with brute strength to labor, doing as I was
   bid;
Living in camps with men-folk, a lonely and loveless
   life;
Never knew kiss of sweetheart, never caress of wife.
A brute with brute strength to labor, and they were
   so far above —
Yet I'd gladly have gone to the gallows for one little
   look of Love.
I, with the strength of two men, savage and shy and
   wild —
Yet how I'd ha' treasured a woman, and the sweet,
   warm kiss of a child!
Well, 'tis Thy world, and Thou knowest. I blaspheme
   and my ways be rude;
But I've lived my life as I found it, and I've done
   my best to be good;
I, the primitive toiler, half naked and grimed to the
   eyes,
Sweating it deep in their ditches, swining it stark in
   their sties;
Hurling down forests before me, spanning
   tumultuous streams;
Down in the ditch building o'er me palaces fairer
   than dreams;
Boring the rock to the ore-bed, driving the road
   through the fen,
Resolute, dumb, uncomplaining, a man in a world
   of men.
Master, I've filled my contract, wrought in Thy
   many lands;

## THE SONG OF THE WAGE-SLAVE

Not by my sins wilt Thou judge me, but by the work
   of my hands.
Master, I've done Thy bidding, and the light is low
   in the west,
And the long, long shift is over ... Master, I've
   earned it — Rest.

# The Wanderlust

he Wanderlust has lured me
    to the seven lonely seas,
Has dumped me on the tailing-piles
    of dearth;
The Wanderlust has haled me from
    the morris chair of ease,
Has hurled me to the ends of all the earth.
How bitterly I've cursed it, oh, the Painted Desert knows,
The wraithlike heights that hug the pallid plain,
The all-but-fluid silence, — yet the longing grows and grows,
And I've got to glut the Wanderlust again.

Soldier, sailor, in what a plight I've been!
Tinker, tailor, oh what a sight I've seen!
And I'm hitting the trail in the morning, boys,
And you won't see my heels for dust;
For it's "all day" with you
When you answer the cue
    Of the Wan-der-lust.

The Wanderlust has got me ... by the belly-aching fire,
By the fever and the freezing and the pain;
By the darkness that just drowns you, by the wail of home desire,
I've tried to break the spell of it — in vain.
Life might have been a feast for me, now there are only crumbs;
In rags and tatters, beggar-wise I sit;
Yet there's no rest or peace for me, imperious it drums,
The Wanderlust, and I must follow it.

## THE WANDERLUST

Highway, by-way, many a mile I've done;
Rare way, fair way, many a height I've won;
But I'm pulling my freight in the morning, boys,
And it's over the hills or bust;
For there's never a cure
When you list to the lure
          Of the Wan-der-lust.

The Wanderlust has taught me ... it has whispered to my heart
Things all you stay-at-homes will never know.
The white man and the savage are but three short days apart,
Three days of cursing, crawling, doubt and woe.
Then it's down to chewing muclucs, to the water you can *eat*,
To fish you bolt with nose held in your hand.
When you get right down to cases, it's King's Grub that rules the races,
And the Wanderlust will help you understand.

Haunting, taunting, that is the spell of it;
Mocking, baulking, that is the hell of it;
But I'll shoulder my pack in the morning, boys,
And I'm going because I must;
For it's so-long to all
When you answer the call
          Of the Wan-der-lust.

The Wanderlust has blest me ... in a ragged blanket curled,
I've watched the gulf of Heaven foam with stars;
I've walked with eyes wide open to the wonder of the world,
I've seen God's flood of glory burst its bars.
I've seen the gold a-blinding in the riffles of the sky,
Till I fancied me a bloated plutocrat;
But I'm freedom's happy bond-slave, and I will be till I die,
And I've got to thank the Wanderlust for that.

## THE WANDERLUST

Wild heart, child heart, all of the world your home.
Glad heart, mad heart, what can you do but roam?
Oh, I'll beat it once more in the morning, boys,
With a pinch of tea and a crust;
For you cannot deny
When you hark to the cry
        Of the Wan-der-lust.

The Wanderlust will claim me at the finish for its own.
I'll turn my back on men and face the Pole.
Beyond the Arctic outposts I will venture all alone;
Some Never-never Land will be my goal.
Thank God! there's none will miss me, for I've been a bird of flight;
And in my moccasins I'll take my call;
For the Wanderlust has ruled me,
And the Wanderlust has schooled me,
And I'm ready for the darkest trail of all.

Grim land, dim land, oh, how the vastness calls!
Far land, star land, oh, how the stillness falls!
For you never can tell if it's heaven or hell,
And I'm taking the trail on trust;
But I haven't a doubt
That my soul will leap out
        On its Wan-der-lust.

# The Joy of Being Poor

## 1

Let others sing of gold and gear,
  the joy of being rich;
But oh, the days when I was poor,
  a vagrant in a ditch!
When every dawn was like a gem,
  so radiant and rare,
And I had but a single coat, and not a single care;
When I would feast right royally on bacon, bread and beer,
And dig into a stack of hay and doze like any peer;
When I would wash beside a brook my solitary shirt,
And though it dried upon my back I never took a hurt;
When I went romping down the road contemptuous of care,
And slapped Adventure on the back — by Gad! we were a pair;
When, though my pockets lacked a coin, and though my coat was old,
The largess of the stars was mine, and all the sunset gold;
When time was only made for fools, and free as air was I,
And hard I hit and hard I lived beneath the open sky;
When all the roads were one to me, and each had its allure ...
Ye Gods! these were the happy days, the days when I was poor.

## 2

Or else, again, old pal of mine, do you recall the times
You struggled with your storyettes, I wrestled with my rhymes;
Oh, we were happy, were we not? — we used to live so "high"
(A little bit of broken roof between us and the sky);
Upon the forge of art we toiled with hammer and with tongs;
You told me all your ripping yarns, I sang to you my songs.
Our hats were frayed, our jackets patched, our boots were down at heel,
But oh, the happy men were we, although we lacked a meal.
And if I sold a bit of rhyme, or if you placed a tale,
What feasts we had of tenderloins and apple-tarts and ale!

161

THE JOY OF BEING POOR

And yet how often we would dine as cheerful as you please,
Beside our little friendly fire on coffee, bread and cheese.
We lived upon the ragged edge, and grub was never sure,
But oh, these were the happy days, the days when we were poor.

## 3

Alas! old man, we're wealthy now, it's sad beyond a doubt;
We cannot dodge prosperity, success has found us out.
Your eye is very dull and drear, my brow is creased with care,
We realize how hard it is to be a millionaire.
The burden's heavy on our backs — you're thinking of your rents,
I'm worrying if I'll invest in five or six per cents.
We've limousines, and marble halls, and flunkeys by the score,
We play the part ... but say, old chap, oh, isn't it a bore?
We work like slaves, we eat too much, we put on evening dress;
We've everything a man can want, I think ... but happiness.

Come, let us sneak away, old chum; forget that we are rich,
And earn an honest appetite, and scratch an honest itch.
Let's be two jolly garreteers, up seven flights of stairs,
And wear old clothes and just pretend we aren't millionaires;
And wonder how we'll pay the rent, and scribble ream on ream,
And sup on sausages and tea, and laugh and loaf and dream.

And when we're tired of that, my friend, oh, you will come with me;
And we will seek the sunlit roads that lie beside the sea.
We'll know the joy the gipsy knows, the freedom nothing mars,
The golden treasure-gates of dawn, the mintage of the stars.
We'll smoke our pipes and watch the pot, and feed the crackling fire,
And sing like two old jolly boys, and dance to heart's desire;
We'll climb the hill and ford the brook and camp upon the moor ...
Old chap, let's haste, I'm mad to taste the Joy of Being Poor.

# A Song of Success

o! we were strong, we were
swift, we were brave.
Youth was a challenge,
and Life was a fight.
All that was best in us
gladly we gave,
Sprang from the rally, and leapt for the height.
Smiling is Love in a foam of Spring flowers:
Harden our hearts to him — on let us press!
Oh, what a triumph and pride shall be ours!
See where it beacons, the star of success!

Cares seem to crowd on us — so much to do;
New fields to conquer, and time's on the wing.
Grey hairs are showing, a wrinkle or two;
Somehow our footstep is losing its spring.
Pleasure's forsaken us, Love ceased to smile;
Youth has been funeralled; Age travels fast.
Sometimes we wonder: is it worth while?
There! we have gained to the summit at last.

Aye, we have triumphed! Now must we haste,
Revel in victory ... why! what is wrong?
Life's choicest vintage is flat to the taste —
Are we too late? Have we laboured too long?
Wealth, power, fame we hold ... ah! but the truth:
Would we not give this vain glory of ours
For one mad, glad year of glorious youth,
Life in the Springtide, and Love in the flowers.

# The Butcher

hey say that
ruthless
Robespierre,
That "sea-green
incorruptible,"
To whom the nobs of nobles were
    By guillotines deductible, —
With necks of dukes at his demand
    Could peel an orange with one hand.

I've tried to do only twice,
    But though the oranges were Sèville,
I made a mush that wasn't nice,
    And damned old Robbie to the devil:
Well, in the end he went, by heck!
    For he, too, got it in the neck.

Aye, finally he lost his nob:
    ('Twas his pet "Maiden" did the chopping)
— I'm glad that was the last of Rob,
    But though the work he did was "topping,"
His triumph was, I understand,
    To peel an orange with one hand.

# Duello

A Frenchman and an
Englishman
Resolved to fight
a duel,
And hit upon a
savage plan,
Because their hate was cruel.
They each would fire a single shot
In room of darkness pitchy,
And who was killed or who was not
Would hang on fingers twitchy.

The room was bare and dark as death,
And each ferocious fighter
Could hear his fierce opponent's breath
And clutched his pistol tighter.
Then Gaston fired — the bullet hissed
On its destructive mission ...
"Thank God!" said John Bull. "He has missed."
The Frenchman cried: "Perdition!"

Then silence followed like a spell,
And as the Briton sought to
Reply he wondered where the hell
His Gallic foe had got to.
And then he thought: "I'll mercy show,
Since Hades is a dire place
To send a fellow to — and so
I'll blaze up through the fireplace."

## DUELLO

So up the chimney he let fly,
Of grace a gallant henchman;
When lo! a sudden, sooty cry,
And down there crashed the Frenchman ...
But if this yarn in France you tell,
Although its vein be skittish,
I think it might be just as well
To make your Frenchman — British.

# Laughter

I laugh at Life: its antics make for
    me a giddy game,
Where only foolish fellows take
    themselves with solemn aim.
I laugh at pomp and vanity, at
    riches, rank and pride;
At social inanity, at swagger, swank and side.
At poets, pastry-cooks and kings, at folk sublime and small,
Who fuss about a thousand things that matter not at all;
At those who dream of name and fame, at those who scheme for pelf....
But best of all the laughing game — is laughing at myself.

Some poet chap has labelled man the noblest work of God:
I see myself a charlatan, a humbug and a fraud.
Yea, 'spite of show and shallow wit, and sentimental drool,
I know myself a hypocrite, a coward and a fool.
And though I kick myself with glee profoundly on the pants,
I'm little worse, it seems to me, than other human ants.
For if you probe your private mind, impervious to shame,
Oh, Gentle Reader, you may find you're much about the same.

Then let us mock with ancient mirth this comic, cosmic plan;
The stars are laughing at the earth; God's greatest joke is man.
For laughter is a buckler bright, and scorn a shining spear;
So let us laugh with all our might at folly, fraud and fear.
Yet on our sorry selves be spent our most sardonic glee.
Oh don't pay life the compliment to take it *seriously*.
For he who can himself despise, be surgeon to the bone,
May win to worth in others' eyes, to wisdom in his own.

# It Is Later Than You Think

Lone amid the
café's cheer,
Sad of heart am
I to-night;
Dolefully I drink
my beer,
But no single line I write.
There's the wretched rent to pay,
Yet I glower at pen and ink:
Oh, inspire me, Muse, I pray,
*It is later than you think!*

Hello! there's a pregnant phrase.
Bravo! let me write it down;
Hold it with a hopeful gaze,
Gauge it with a fretful frown;
Tune it to my lyric lyre ...
Ah! upon starvation's brink,
How the words are dark and dire:
It is later than you think.

Weigh them well.... Behold yon band,
Students drinking by the door,
Madly merry, *bock* in hand,
Saucers stacked to mark their score.
Get you gone, you jolly scamps;
Let your parting glasses clink;
Seek your long neglected lamps:
It is later than you think.

## IT IS LATER THAN YOU THINK

Look again: yon dainty blonde,
All allure and golden grace,
Oh so willing to respond
Should you turn a smiling face.
Play your part, poor pretty doll;
Feast and frolic, pose and prink;
There's the Morgue to end it all,
And it's later than you think.

Yon's a playwright — mark his face,
Puffed and purple, tense and tired;
Pasha-like he holds his place,
Hated, envied and admired.
How you gobble life, my friend;
Wine, and woman soft and pink!
Well, each tether has its end:
Sir, it's later than you think.

See yon living scarecrow pass
With a wild and wolfish stare
At each empty absinthe glass,
As if he saw Heaven there.
Poor damned wretch, to end your pain
There is still the Greater Drink.
Yonder waits the sanguine Seine ...
It is later than you think.

## IT IS LATER THAN YOU THINK

Lastly, you who read; aye, you
Who this very line may scan:
Think of all you planned to do ...
Have you done the best you can?
See! the tavern lights are low;
Black's the night, and how you shrink!
God! and is it time to go?
Ah! the clock is always slow;
It is later than you think;
Sadly later than you think;
Far, far later than you think.

# My Highland Home

y mother spun
    the household wool,
And all our kiddy
    clothes would make;
I used to go barefoot
    to school,
  While bannock took the place of cake.
One shirt a week was all I had,
  Our home was just a but-and-ben;
But oh I was the proudful lad,
  And life was rich with promise then.

Although I supped on milk and brose,
  And went to bed by candle-light,
I pored on books of noble prose,
  And longed like Bobbie Burns to write.
Now in this age of the machine
  I look back three-score years and ten:
With life so simple, sane and clean,
  Oh were we not more happy then?

We deemed not of electric light,
  Nor ever thought that we would fly;
Our sons were not called up to fight,
  And in a foreign field to die.
So now when threats of war appal,
  And millions cower to monster men,
Friends, don't you think that, after all,
  We were a heap more happy then?

# Repentance

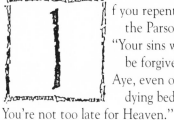f you repent,"
the Parson said,
"Your sins will
be forgiven.
Aye, even on your
dying bed
You're not too late for Heaven."

That's just my cup of tea, I thought,
Though for my sins I sorrow;
Since salvation is easy brought
I will repent . . . to-morrow.

To-morrow and to-morrow went,
But though my youth was flying,
I was reluctant to repent,
Having no fear of dying.

'Tis plain, I mused, the more I sin,
(To Satan's jubilation)
When I repent the more I'll win
Celestial approbation.

So still I sin, and though I fail
To get snow-whitely shriven,
My timing's good: I hope to hail
The last bus up to Heaven.

# Nature Man

he happiest man
    I ever knew
Was scarcely
    clad at all;
He had no bath
    like me and you,
  But owned a waterfall.
And every sunrise he would wade
  The streamlet silver bright,
To stand beneath the clear cascade
    With sheer delight.

The happiest man I ever knew
  Lived in a forest glade;
His hut of palm-leaf and bamboo
  With his own hands he made.
And for his breakfast he would pick
  A bread-fruit from the tree,
Or lobster he would gaily flick
    From out the sea.

The happiest man I ever knew
  Could barely read or write,
But beer from honey he could brew
  To get drunk every night.
He had no wife as I'm aware,
  Nor any bastard brat,
But lived a life without a care,
    With laughter fat.

## NATURE MAN

The happiest man I ever knew
    Was innocent of rent;
Low labour he would scorn to do
    And never owned a cent.
But he would strum an old guitar
    And sing a sultry song,
Insouciant as children are
      Of right and wrong.

The happiest man I ever knew
    Recked not of government;
His wants were simple and so few
    His life was pure content.
And as I thole this rancid mart,
    In which I plot and plan,
How glad I'd be, with all my heart,
      That happy man.

# Pantheist

 olling on
a bank
of thyme
Drunk with
Spring I made
this rhyme....

Though peoples perish in defeat,
And races suffer to survive,
The sunshine never was so sweet,
So vast the joy to be alive;
The laughing leaves, the glowing grass
Proclaim how good it is to be;
The pines are lyric as I pass,
The hills hosannas sing to me.

Pink roses ring yon placid palm,
Soft shines the blossom of the peach;
The sapphire sea is satin calm,
With bell-like tinkle on the beach;
A lizard lazes in the sun,
A bee is bumbling to my hand;
Shy breezes whisper: "You are one
With us because you understand."

PANTHEIST

Yea, I am one with all I see,
With wind and wave, with pine and palm;
Their very elements in me
Are fused to make me what I am.
Through me their common life-stream flows,
And when I yield this human breath,
In leaf and blossom, bud and rose,
Live on I will ... There is no Death.

Oh, let me flee from woeful things,
And listen to the linnet's song;
To solitude my spirit clings,
To sunny woodlands I belong.
O foolish men! Yourselves destroy,
But I from pain would win surcease....
O Earth, grant me eternal joy!
O Nature — everlasting peace!

                                        Amen.

# Moderation

hat pious people
label vice
I reckon mainly
pleasure;
I deem that women,
wine and dice
Are good in modest measure;
Though sanctity and truth receive
My hearty approbation,
Of all the virtues, I believe
The best is Moderation.

Be moderate in love and hate,
Soft pedal on emotion;
And never let your passion get
The better of your caution.
Should Right or Leftist seek to goad
You from the course that's level,
Stick to the middle of the road
And send them to the devil.

Though rich the feast be moderate
In eating and in drinking;
An appetite insatiate
Is evil to my thinking.
Though ladies languidly await
Your kisses, on your way shun
Their wiles, but — well, be moderate
Even in moderation.

## MODERATION

Avoid extremes: be moderate
   In saving and in spending;
An equable and easy gait
   Will win an easy ending....
So here's to him of open mind,
   Of sense and toleration,
That hope of headlong human-kind,
   The Man of Moderation.

# Inspiration

How often have
I started out
With no thought
in my noddle,
And wandered here
and there about,
Where fancy bade me toddle;
Till feeling faunlike in my glee
I've voiced some gay distiches,
Returning joyfully to tea,
A poem in my britches.

A-squatting on a thymy slope
With vast of sky about me,
I've scribbled on an envelope
The rhymes the hills would shout me;
The couplets that the trees would call,
The lays the breezes proffered . . .
Oh no, I didn't *think* at all —
I took what Nature offered.

For that's the way you ought to write —
Without a trace of trouble;
Be super-charged with high delight
And let the words out-bubble;
Be voice of vale and wood and stream
Without design or proem:
Then rouse from out a golden dream
To find you've made a poem.

## INSPIRATION

So I'll go forth with mind a blank,
And sea and sky will spell me;
And lolling on a thymy bank
I'll take down what they tell me;
As Mother Nature speaks to me
Her words I'll gaily docket,
So I'll come singing home to tea
A poem in my pocket.

# Facility

So easy 'tis to
 make a rhyme,
That did the world
 but know it,
Your coachman might
 Parnassus climb,
Your butler be a poet.

Then, oh, how charming it would be
If, when in haste hysteric
You called the page, you learned that he
Was grappling with a lyric.

Or else what rapture it would yield,
When cook sent up the salad,
To find within its depths concealed
A touching little ballad.

Or if for tea and toast you yearned,
What joy to find upon it
The chambermaid had coyly laid
A palpitating sonnet.

Your baker could the fashion set;
Your butcher might respond well;
With every tart a triolet,
With every chop a rondel.

## FACILITY

Your tailor's bill ... well, I'll be blowed!
Dear chap! I never knowed him ...
He's gone and written me an ode,
Instead of what I *owed* him.

So easy 'tis to rhyme ... yet stay!
Oh, terrible misgiving!
Please do not give the game away ...
I've got to make my living.

# Pullman Porter

he porter in the
Pullman car
Was charming, as they
sometimes are.
He scanned my baggage
tags: "Are you
The man who wrote of Lady Lou?"
When I said "yes" he made a fuss —
Oh, he was most assiduous;
And I was pleased to think that he
Enjoyed my brand of poetry.

He was forever at my call,
So when we got to Montreal
And he had brushed me off, I said:
"I'm glad my poems you have read,
I feel quite flattered, I confess,
And if you give me your address
I'll send you (autographed, of course)
One of my little books of verse."

He smiled — his teeth were white as milk;
He spoke — his voice was soft as silk.
I recognized, despite his skin,
The perfect gentleman within.
Then courteously he made reply:
"I thank you kindly, Sir, but I
With many other cherished tome
Have all your books of verse at home.

## PULLMAN PORTER

"When I was quite a little boy
I used to savour them with joy;
And now my daughter, aged three,
Can tell the tale of Sam McGee;
While Tom, my son, that's only two,
Has heard the yarn of Dan McGrew....
Don't think your stuff I'm not applaudin' —
My taste is Eliot and Auden."

So as we gravely bade adieu
I felt quite snubbed — and so would you.
And yet I shook him by the hand,
Impressed that he could understand
The works of those two tops I mention,
So far beyond *my* comprehension —
A humble bard of boys and barmen,
Disdained, alas! by Pullman carmen.

# My Masterpiece

It's slim and trim
   and bound in blue;
Its leaves are crisp and
   edged with gold;
Its words are simple,
   stalwart too;
Its thoughts are tender, wise and bold.
Its pages scintillate with wit;
Its pathos clutches at my throat:
Oh, how I love each line of it!
That Little Book I Never Wrote.

In dreams I see it praised and prized
By all, from plowman unto peer;
It's pencil-marked and memorized,
It's loaned (and not returned, I fear);
It's worn and torn and travel-tossed,
And even dusky natives quote
That classic that the world has lost,
The Little Book I Never Wrote.

Poor ghost! For homes you've failed to cheer,
For grieving hearts uncomforted,
Don't haunt me now.... Alas! I fear
The fire of Inspiration's dead.
A humdrum way I go to-night,
From all I hoped and dreamed remote:
Too late ... a better man must write
That Little Book I Never Wrote.

# The Three Voices

he waves have a
    story to tell me,
As I lie on the
    lonely beach;
Chanting aloft in
    the pine-tops,
The wind has a lesson to teach;
But the stars sing an anthem of glory
    I cannot put into speech.

The waves tell of ocean spaces,
    Of hearts that are wild and brave,
Of populous city places,
    Of desolate shores they lave,
Of men who sally in quest of gold
    To sink in an ocean grave.

The wind is a mighty roamer;
    He bids me keep me free,
Clean from the taint of the gold-lust,
    Hardy and pure as he;
Cling with my love to nature,
    As a child to the mother-knee.

But the stars throng out in their glory,
    And they sing of the God in man;
They sing of the Mighty Master,
    Of the loom his fingers span,
Where a star or a soul is a part of the whole,
    And weft in the wondrous plan.

## THE THREE VOICES

Here by the camp-fire's flicker,
    Deep in my blanket curled,
I long for the peace of the pine-gloom,
    When the scroll of the Lord is unfurled,
And the wind and the wave are silent,
    And world is singing to world.

# L'Envoi

We talked of yesteryears,
 of trails and treasure,
Of men who played the
 game and lost or won;
Of mad stampedes, of toil
 beyond all measure,
 Of camp-fire comfort when the day was done.
We talked of sullen nights by moon-dogs haunted,
 Of bird and beast and tree, of rod and gun;
Of boat and tent, of hunting-trip enchanted
 Beneath the wonder of the midnight sun;
Of bloody-footed dogs that gnawed the traces,
 Of prisoned seas, wind-lashed and winter-locked;
The ice-gray dawn was pale upon our faces,
 Yet still we filled the cup and still we talked.

The city street was dimmed. We saw the glitter
 Of moon-picked brilliants on the virgin snow,
And down the drifted canyon heard the bitter,
 Relentless slogan of the winds of woe.
The city was forgot, and, parka-skirted,
 We trod that leagueless land that once we knew;
We saw stream past, down valleys glacier-girted,
 The wolf-worn legions of the caribou.
We smoked our pipes, o'er scenes of triumph dwelling,
 Of deeds of daring, dire defeats, we talked;
And other tales that lost not in the telling,
 Ere to our beds uncertainly we walked.

## L'ENVOI

And so, dear friends, in gentler valleys roaming,
   Perhaps, when on my printed page you look,
Your fancies by the firelight may go homing
   To that lone land that haply you forsook.
And if perchance you hear the silence calling,
   The frozen music of star-yearning heights,
Or, dreaming, see the seines of silver trawling
   Across the sky's abyss on vasty nights,
You may recall that sweep of savage splendor,
   That land that measures each man at his worth.
And feel in memory, half fierce, half tender,
   The brotherhood of men that know the North.

# Index of First Lines